FOR A BETTER W

A SOCIAL ACTION GUIDE FOR CHRISTIANS

FOR A BETTER WORLD

A SOCIAL ACTION GUIDE FOR CHRISTIANS

Richard Adams

Phil Wells

Extra research and material by
Iris Webb

LYNX

Published by
Lynx Communications
Sandy Lane West, Oxford, England
ISBN 0 7459 2682 7

An imprint of Lion Publishing plc

First edition 1994

A catalogue record for this book is available
from the British Library

Printed and bound in Malta

CONTENTS

FOREWORD

We were amazed to find, as we began research for this book, that no study guide on contemporary issues was available for Christian groups. This volume only partly meets that need. Important areas of daily living, like health, education and the way personal relationships are seen in today's world, are only touched on in passing. But we believe the seven topics chosen will provide much to discuss. More importantly, we hope the way we have suggested you approach them will be applied to other topics of your choice. Please let us know how you use the book and how your group reacts to it.

Richard and Phil would like to thank Iris for helping out when time was tight and, in doing so, adding a great deal and substantially enhancing the work. Our thanks also to Catharine Howe, without whom, as they say, this book would not have been possible. There are many omissions, particularly in our lists of books, resources and organizations, and we regret that the broad remit made this inevitable. The errors and opinions we hope are distinguishable from each other, but both are our own.

Richard Adams, Phil Wells, Iris Webb

HOW TO USE THE GUIDE

This guide is unusual in several respects. Unlike a normal study guide, it is not designed to be used in a logical way, from start to finish. In fact, our hope is that you'll never get to the end. It is an action/study guide, designed to enable and encourage Christian groups—house groups, study groups, social concern groups—to become involved in meeting the many needs in our society. We'd all like to be better at meeting needs, and we'd also like to be better informed. This guide will help us to do both.

Talking to, working with, learning from people who are meeting needs—and the many people our society is hurting; finding ways to overcome the barriers; seeing things from the 'underside'; discovering resources within ourselves and from elsewhere, and ways of using them; finding people whose lives are enriched by meeting the needs of others: these are all key ways to free ourselves from the 'me-first' culture we are exposed to day to day.

The guide is organized into several broad areas of concern; some you will be drawn to, others you will not. Our hope is that you will use this guide to explore your concerns and set your priorities as individuals and as a group, based on those of the Bible and the body of Christ at large. We hope that, having decided on an area of need you wish to engage in, you will reflect together on the concern and your experiences; and commit yourself to some small action. The process of action—reflection—further action may mean that you never look at the rest of the guide. It is designed to be flexible and meet your objectives, not to compose a programme of study and stimulus.

A further—and important—difference between this and other guides is that it is not a recipe book. It attempts to stimulate thinking, discussion and decision making, but does not give agendas and outlines for meetings. For one thing, the guide is for use by existing groups, with established ways of working together: how you use it is up to you. And besides, how you work will depend on your own resources and experience.

The key to the guide is this introduction; it is about setting the agenda for your group. It uses a collection of quotations to stimulate thinking and discussion, suggests a bible study to root the discussion into the teaching of Christ, the early church and the prophets, and provides some ideas to help your group to set its priorities and take the first vital step into action. The other elements comprising the introductory section of the guide are:

'**Christians and Social Action**': images from the history of the church as it has changed the world, again in the form of short passages and quotations. This can be dipped into by individuals and then shared in the group, if that would be helpful.

'**Tools at our Disposal**': a survey of the main ways we can (and already do) influence the world at home, work or school, in our neighbourhoods, the country and the world. This introduces the main themes, and specific ideas will be developed in each section.

'**Addresses**': simply a list of the places you can get help, when you come to take action.

The remaining chapters of the guide each

concentrate on one area of concern, be it Poverty, the Environment, Consumer Culture, or Violence and Peace. Each is arranged in a similar form:

'What's up?': a brief survey of the issue, so that all group members get an overview of the area of concern. This is in the form of short passages and quotations to read and share.

'Group Discussion': just as in the introduction, a collection of readings and discussion points, and a short Bible study, to help the group decide where to focus its efforts.

'Actions and Possibilities': a collection of ideas and examples drawn from the successes (and failures) of other groups concerned about the issue.

'Organizations and resources': what might help, who to join or work together with, and where to go.

INTRODUCTION:
CHRISTIANS AND SOCIAL ACTION

This guide begs an important question: should Christians be involved in society, in social change? Throughout history, there have been many who have believed so. Jesus' own view seems straightforward: 'Anything you did not do for one of these, however humble, you did not do for me.' Yet there is, and always has been, another perspective, also based on the teaching of Jesus: 'My kingdom is not of this world,' and we are advised not to give much thought to tomorrow, what we should eat or wear. So why be concerned about social issues?

Doing justice is not the application of our religious faith. It is its very substance. For, as the biblical prophet Jeremiah has told us, to do justice is to know God. (Jeremiah 22:13–16)

Kathleen and James McGinnis,
Parenting for Peace and Justice

Firstly, faith without works is dead. The 'works' concerned are not just a token of faith but the response of the whole person. 'But if anyone has the world's goods and sees his brother in need, yet closes his heart against him, how does God's love abide in him?' (1 John 3:17). Neither should faith become synonymous with piety: 'Turn your eyes upon Jesus/ Look full in his wonderful face/ And the things of earth will grow strangely dim/ In the light of his glory and grace.' This division of life into 'spiritual' and 'physical' realms is not mainstream to the Bible. There's every sign that 'the things of earth' were sharply in focus for Jesus; no one accused him of being no earthly use.

There is a strong imperative from the Bible to raise questions about our society, about how it treats the poor and the people it leaves out.

David Jenkins in Christians in Britain Today

Bishop David Jenkins' view of the importance of social concern is founded on the nature of God:

Firstly, God is the creator of, involved with and concerned about everything, so faith in him cannot be confined to a part of life, falsely labelled 'spiritual', private and individual. Secondly, God, Jesus and the Bible are all about love, and this means about people and relationships. If you put these two together, you are bound as a Christian to be concerned about the material conditions that affect people, the relationships between people and therefore the structures and institutions that affect people and that is how you get into politics.

Christians in Britain Today

While God's love does not distinguish between the spiritual and the physical well-being of his creatures, the apparent divide inherent in Jesus' teaching on taking no thought for tomorrow is bridged by the fact that it is in God that we must trust. Pursuing 'earthly' targets of wealth or fame are seen as idolatry; a worship of false gods. Yet it is this very spiritual problem that gives rise to many of the physical problems the prophets rail against.

If we idolise wealth, then we create poverty; if we idolise success, then we create the inadequate; if we idolise power, then we create powerlessness.

Thomas Cullinan OSB

According to author and pastor Jim Wallis, 'Again and again in the scriptures, the exploitation and suffering of the poor is directly attributed to the substitution of the worship of mammon for the true worship of God.' Yet in the early church, as today, people could not recognize idolatry in themselves. John Chrysostom, a fourth century patriarch, criticized the rich who came to church, prayed to God and carried out 'all the duties of a Christian': 'You pretend to be serving God, but in reality you have submitted yourself to the hard and galling yoke of ruthless greed.'

For the triumph of evil, it is only necessary that good men do nothing.

Edmund Burke

In the beatitudes, in his healing and prophetic ministry, and in the very fact of his incarnation, Jesus wove the spiritual and physical into a seamless garment, perhaps most clearly expressed in his teaching of the kingdom, breaking into the present age, echoing the Old Testament idea of Shalom. While it is normally translated as 'peace', *shalom* refers to the well-being of a community at peace, where right relationships between people and their God ensure that there is no weeping or suffering. This is not just pie in the sky; Jesus emphasized that shalom is to be pursued here and now, as well.

This has been implicitly recognized by individual Christians who, faced by need, know 'what Jesus would do', or know what the kingdom is about; all the formulations boil down to the character of God, revealed in the everyday actions of Christians. But it has also been recognized more publicly by evangelistic

leaders over many years. While there has been a dispute over whether evangelism or social action is the proper duty of a Christian, such a question does not characterize the ministries of Wesley, Shaftesbury or Wilberforce. Charles Finney, the father of modern evangelism, was so concerned about the social issue of slavery that he went as far as to deny slave owners communion, saying that is was impossible for the church to take a neutral stance on such social issues. If the church fails to speak out, 'she is perjured, and the spirit of God departs from her'. In the call to conversion:

We must constantly remind ourselves that we are part of that system [held responsible for the world's problems] by the way in which we live. Structural injustice exists because of our demands, with our assent, because of our failure to stand up and witness to God's law.

Barbara Wood, Our World, God's World

The dichotomy between social involvement and separation has riven the evangelical tradition in particular for decades, though it was resolved by the International Congress on World Evangelization in 1974 (the Lausanne Covenant): 'When people receive Christ they are born again into his kingdom and must seek not only to exhibit but also to spread its righteousness in the midst of an unrighteous world. The salvation we claim should be transforming us in the totality of our personal and social responsibility. Faith without works is dead.'

WHAT IS SOCIAL ACTION?

There was once a factory in which industrial injuries were common. Local Christians, concerned at the suffering and occasional deaths, decided to establish a first aid post at the factory gate. Here people could get immediate treatment and many limbs and lives were saved. The factory owner was supportive; he donated money for medicine and equipment and even allowed the first aid post to set up in a spare room in the factory. But people were still injured; some still died. Some of the workers could not understand why the Christians did not confront the factory owner and suggest investing in safer equipment, or lobby the local government for legislation to improve safety. Social action means works of mercy (direct service) to help those in need or to make the world a better place. But it also means works of justice (social change) to address some of the causes of poverty, suffering or environmental decay. The church finds the first much easier, because it doesn't ask awkward questions, or demand any changes that might affect the way we live.

The Bible is often held to bar Christians from involvement in social change, and political work in particular; the injunction being to obey earthly authorities instituted by God. Yet, of course, authorities are roundly condemned by the prophets, and were disobeyed by early Christians on matters of principle. Indeed, the early Christians were regarded as an underground movement by the governments of the day. Living in a democracy gives us the urgent task to ensure that governments do carry out their primary objective in terms of Christian duty; the protection of the weak.

This point was not lost on John Newton, whose job was to transport slaves to the New World. On his conversion, he stopped dealing in slaves, became a church leader and wrote one of the most famous hymns, 'Amazing Grace'. But, more significantly, he led the campaign against slavery, with the reformer Wilberforce.

WHY ARE CHRISTIANS NOT MORE ACTIVE?

There are of course many reasons, apart from the unease about social involvement felt by some. While the Bible is clear about the principles that underlie the way society should run, the practical implications are not always clear. Added to this we are often ignorant; while we may be aware of many social and

environmental problems, we feel we don't know enough about them to act, or enough about what actions to take; and we lack imagination.

Even when it is clear to us what to do, we are still less involved in society than we would like to be. We have a mixture of feelings: not enough time left once the daily chores are done and the kids are in bed, perhaps; a fear of getting in 'over our heads', becoming embroiled in something we cannot back out of; a feeling that there are so many issues, too complex and too large for us to make a difference.

This guide seeks to address just these problems. We can work together in groups to motivate and support one another; find hidden resources and sources of help; become involved in a small way and begin to see what can be done; and gain a deeper understanding of the need. This is the ground we will cover. Fundamentally, like Christianity itself, this book is empowering.

Barbara Wood put her finger on a deeper issue:

For many people, living ordinary, blameless lives, it is difficult to respond to God's call to repentance because it is hard to recognize what our sins are and, therefore, to feel that true deep sorrow and desire for change. Today we are called to recognize that sin has pervaded all our actions, that our very life-style is an act of rebellion against God's love. We can no longer look at sin as a private matter between ourselves and God, and blame the evils of the world on governments, industry, the feckless poor and the countless other scapegoats we have been accustomed to hold responsible. It is a matter for each one of us to respond to and recognize our responsibility as individuals and as members of one another.'
Barbara Wood, Our World, God's World

Also in each section, we will explore ways in which we are involved in society, for good or ill, and at ways in which our 'conversion' can be made concrete in our lives.

TOOLS AT OUR DISPOSAL

One of the abiding problems for anyone concerned about social action is finding the time. By the time we have done the household chores, put the kids to bed, we rarely seem to have time even for a meeting to discuss the issue, let alone to decide to take action. But Christianity is not about what we do between eight and ten each evening, and if our faith has something to say about the world then it has to say it in real life, not in the optional extras. In this section, we look at several areas of life and at the way we already influence the world we live in and will leave to the next generation. We will also introduce some of the ways in which we can change things for good.

IN THE HOME

The household is the basic forum for all social action. The way we spend our money, the way we relate to each other, the way we raise children (and the way children influence their parents!) and the way we express our faith all have implications for the society and the world around us. But while today we live out much of our lives in the context of the household, we have lost much of the support available to previous generations. Households have to be independent and self-sufficient spiritually, psychologically and financially in a way that limits their ability to take risks and to learn to trust in God. Without the extended family, the responsibility lies with the church as a community of faith to provide security.

For the family to fulfil all its potentialities for nurturing open, loving persons free to carry out radically new missions in an aching society, some equivalent of this extended family is necessary. No family can do this alone.
Elise Boulding, in Parenting for Peace and Justice

But the home is also a major resource; we will almost certainly spend more money on this than on anything else, after all. There are many ways in which we can use our home in socially-supportive ways, from providing a home for a foster child or a 'young offender' to providing a base for committee meetings or a food co-op.

CONSUMING

Households have tremendous resources at their disposal. In the UK each year we spend over £400 billion as consumers. We are accustomed to thinking carefully about how much of this we can divert to 'good causes' rather than to sustain our lifestyles, though in a world of need few of us feel happy with the amount we give. But the 90 per cent (or, nationally, the 99 per cent) that we spend on living is another important resource. What products we buy, and which companies we buy from, can make a difference.

The policies of our biggest companies on Third World involvement, equal opportunities, military contracts, community involvement or the environment are vitally important; after governments, they make the biggest decisions. A powerful tool is to buy from—vote for—companies pursuing policies that address some of the big social issues we are concerned about. In the following sections, we can explore what this might mean in practice.

But for Christians, consumerism has a deeper significance; put starkly, Why are we here? We live in a society whose major life goals are concerned with possessing; we are told that to live life to the full we need more and more things. To be secure, we need to ensure that nothing or no one can take those things away. We are told that 'what's mine's me own' to do with as I please, and that if something cannot be given a monetary value, it isn't worth having.

We know that none of this is true, but swimming against the tide of conventional wisdom is hard, and social action, at root, is saying that the non-tradeable 'goods' are the most important: the sense of community, health, self-worth, clean air, relationships, true security, peace . . . shalom.

Kathleen and James McGinnis, in *Parenting for Peace and Justice*, refer to a broader concept of stewardship: developing a greater concern for life—and people—rather than things; 'good times' based on people rather than things; less dependence on possessions and money for happiness and security with greater reliance on one's own insights and abilities; personal growth—greater awareness of our own motivations and unconscious patterns of life. This process of non-conformity is at the root of Christian social action.

CHILDREN

Unless children, at the earliest age, experience their own strength and a feeling of belonging, the opportunity for achieving the fullest measure of freedom with responsibility is lost. Once children become full partners in their family, the foundation of their future life is established, and they become contributing members of their school and society. People's potential can only be realized to its fullest when all human beings are confident of their worth to the society in which they live.

Sadie Dreikurs in *Parenting for Peace and Justice*

We are all formed during childhood, and values created at that stage are hard to change, so bringing up children as caring and active participants is vital. At the same time, it is the raising of children that seems to conflict with so much that we'd like to do: money, time, and taking risks all become more difficult. Kathleen and James McGinnis emphasize the crucial importance of involving children in social action. Their excellent *Parenting for Peace and Justice* forms the basis for the following ideas.

Involve children:
To give them hope that they can change things: based on reality;
To show them that social action is a normal part of life;
To give them the rewards that come from working together;
To promote children's self-esteem and self-confidence;
To help them develop as caring persons;
Because not to act is to be part of the problem;
Because if not you'll have no time for them, or for social action;
Because not to act is not to worship God (Isaiah 58:6–11).

But this involvement has to be voluntary and based on mutual decisions. Parents who opt for voluntary poverty without involving the children will create resentment, for example, and coercion is seldom a way to build enthusiasm! Children benefit most from very concrete action—meeting other people involved, real situations—which increases motivation, and understanding. Activities with a fun element, with a specific role for the children (and other families) will help. Specific ideas will be developed in the following sections.

As with adults, relating social concern to children's developing relationship with God, and broadening their horizons and developing a sense of awe and wonder are suggested as the first steps towards stewardship: integrating prayer and social action. Pray it and do it.

INPUTS

But, like it or not, parents are only one influence upon children, and sometimes it seems, not a major one! The prevailing culture rubs off onto children through television, peer pressure at school and the reading material they are given. Much 'social action' at home will involve looking critically at this culture with its implicit greed, violence, sexism and intolerance. Again, specific ideas will be explored later, but a basic

13

principle is inoculation: trying to shield children from the world is futile; it is also no preparation for life in the world.

The aim is to equip children to come to grips with life on the streets, while giving them the confidence and the tools to hold to another view of the world.

AT WORK OR SCHOOL

For many of us, the home is also the environment in which we work. That presents special problems, which we can explore under some of the 'topics' later. But work outside the home is also a difficult area for Christians. We have to make a living, and while at work we have to do what our employer wants. So is there room for 'Christianity'? A typical response is that a Christian is much the same as anyone, but works harder and more honestly; all work should be done to the glory of God. But can it? In our society, some work may be held to work against some of the values we espouse as Christians. Christianity at work is about choosing the right job, not merely working hard, being honest and saying a word for Jesus now and again.

It is also about what our employers do. The companies we look critically at as consumers, to see what policies they have on the environment or equal opportunities, are also employers. How does your employer rate? What questions could you ask, or what action can you take to make your employer a better citizen?

The same principle holds at school. Schools have an enormous influence on children, and affect the environment, too. Both parents and pupils have opportunities to help the staff and governors to consider social and environmental questions they may never have before.

Some of us operate at the other end: as employers or managers. Many Christians believe that, like politics, it is impossible to 'make it to the top' in business without compromise, or without being swallowed up by the culture. Supporting those who are in leadership in an informed and critical way to help them survive and be creative in the pressures of a foreign culture is a further aspect of social action. In this area it is important to ask, 'What is my church, as a church, doing to support people in their work?' Is there a forum for discussing issues of faith and work? Do we understand what some jobs involve so that we can be constructively supportive?

IN THE COMMUNITY

This is the most obvious forum for local church involvement. The range of actions is very wide, which is perhaps one of the major difficulties as the choice itself is an excuse to put off action. The crucial area to address is matching resources to needs. The needs may not be obvious, especially when so many churches have little contact with local communities, though many churches have done their own research to find out what local people perceive as the priorities. Similarly, the resources available—both within and beyond the church—may not be obvious, and a similar survey may yield some surprising results.

One way to make progress on both these issues is to work through other local organizations. There are many community groups and social action organizations with the knowledge and resources you need. Their agenda may well be different from your own, especially if the group has not got a Christian basis, but this is much the best way to learn approaches, to gain skills and to build commitment. Setting in place an original work may be a later step. In all the following sections, there are pointers to the ways churches can get involved in the local community, with both the 'feet of Christian service' outlined above.

IN THE NATION/THE WORLD

Beyond our own locality, direct involvement is more difficult, though paradoxically, churches are rather better at working at this level. The advantage of 'global' concerns is their very distance; we can put them down when we have had enough; we know we will not get sucked in over our heads. At this level, obvious actions are writing letters to governments, companies and other bodies, and raising money for causes here and overseas.

However, two other avenues exist, which are less well trodden. Raising awareness of national and global issues is important—for its own sake, as well as to stimulate action. Changing the climate of opinion and putting less local issues on the agenda are long-term—but in the last analysis, essential—tasks. The church has a special responsibility to point to the deeper values that underlie many of the assumptions made in our society, and to challenge them. This work can be very public—meetings,

campaigns—or very individual—writing letters to local papers, raising issues within groups we belong to. But all of it is based on informing and supporting one another.

The second avenue to explore is making links. While prayer puts us in touch with the body of Christ—the worldwide family of God— at a spiritual level, actually meeting Christians of other cultures and communities means that we can learn and share more fully. Links which involve a genuine sharing between churches and individuals in different areas or countries can be a stimulus to growth for both. It can also be a costly process as we discover the connections between social problems and our lifestyles—as seen through the eyes of another group.

OUR CONCERNS AND PRIORITIES

Deciding what to do is always a difficult process; like jumping into the water when you don't know the temperature. This section is intended to help groups discover what social and environmental problems concern them most, and to decide which to tackle first.

How you approach the material will depend on the nature of your group: how many decisions you have already taken; how well you know each other; whether or not you have recognized leaders or 'experts', and so on. It would be helpful if one or two people reviewed the whole section and decided how to handle it. Different people could take responsibility for different parts.

A SUGGESTED FORMAT

Individuals may want to read 'Christians and social action' and 'Tools at our disposal' before the group meets for the first time, so that the group has a common starting point.

'Our concerns' may be a useful starting point, especially if the group has not already

decided on a broad area of concern. This will probably occupy one session. If people are short of ideas, the 'Concerns' list can start the ball rolling. Either suggest a few, or write them up randomly and the group can begin to sort them out and build links/add others together.

'Circles of involvement' and 'Group resources survey' fit well together, with part one of the 'Circle' (sorting out priorities) taking one session, and the 'Group resources survey' another: what we can do will depend on our resources. As 'homework' between these sessions, try to list your own resources.

'Looking at the Bible' can slot in at the end, before the plunge, or the group could reflect upon one or two readings at the start of each session.

'Where are we going?' is clearly the jumping-off point and here you are on your own! You can elect to look at one of the topics developed in the Action/Study Guide that matches most closely your priorities.

This session must be based on free discussion, reflection, consensus . . . and prayer.

LOOKING AT THE BIBLE

Alternative perspectives

The Good Samaritan revisited. Read the well-known story (**Luke 10:29–37**) and then ask what would have happened if the Samaritan had arrived while the traveller was being attacked.

Shalom

The vision of wholeness in society and the created order gives us direction and hope. (**Isaiah 65:20–25; Jeremiah 31; Micah 4:3–4**)

The prophets

The big concerns in biblical times were poverty (and what we might call consumerism!), violence and spiritual corruption. All these are illustrated graphically in the book of Amos. With the risk of allowing pet themes and strong feelings to emerge, select two or three passages from Amos and ask if they have relevance today.

Getting involved

We may feel powerless, but God will provide, and our feeling of inadequacy should not be seen as a problem or deterrent. (**Exodus 3; 4:1–17; Matthew 11:30; Romans 12:11–12**)

OUR CONCERNS

This is a ninety-minute group session (including break for coffee).

You'll need pens, paper, a large sheet of paper and large felt pens—depending on numbers.

If there are more than six of you, divide up into small groups, of between three and six. Spend ten minutes or so listing on a sheet of paper all the things that are wrong with the world—and you can include everything!

In groups, spend five minutes sifting the list and trying to arrange these concerns into groups, ready to put up on the 'master list'.

When satisfied, write your revised list up on a large sheet of paper on the wall. Watch what others are doing, and if you can add to someone else's categories, do so. If some of your concerns are already up, you can miss them out.

Spend a few more minutes looking at the completed list in silence, then, in your groups discuss your feelings when you think about these concerns. Make sure each person can respond, and make a note of the different feelings expressed.

After ten or fifteen minutes, come together as a large group and share the feelings you have noted. Someone could write them up next to the list of concerns.

When people have shared enough, allow a short period of silence and then, as a large group, list up all thing things that give you hope in the face of all these problems. Try not to discuss them, just shout out and write up.

You may want to finish with a silent reflection and/or open prayer on the ways in which we are both part of the problem and of the solution.

Remember that many people are worried about 'negative' feelings, such as anger and despair. Like the awareness of our own failings, these are signs of hope—the Spirit's work within us. *Not* to have such feelings in the face of greed, suffering and hate would be much more worrying.

Reading the Bible is more dangerous than we often would like it to be. It puts us under an obligation.

Conrad Boerma

CONCERNS

You may like to use the following list to prompt or stimulate response. It is not meant to be definitive and you will find several issues of importance to your group that are not included.

Abortion	Advertising	Aids	Arms spending	Biotechnology
Child abuse	Children	Community	Consumerism	Crime
Debt	Disability	Disadvantage	Dishonesty	Education
Environment	Equal opportunities	Euthanasia	Family breakdown	Food
Freedoms	Genetic diversity	Greed	Health	Homelessness
Human rights	Immigration	Inner city	Intolerance	Literacy
Loneliness	Marginalization	Media	Mental illness	Money
Nationalism	Nuclear arms	Old age	Peace	Penal reform
Politics	Pollution	Population	Pornography	Poverty
Prostitution	Racism	Refugees	Religion	Resources
Sexism	Sexuality	Single people	Slavery	Substance abuse
Third World	Trade	Training	Transport	Unemployment
Violence	War	Waste	Women	World order
Young people				

CIRCLES OF INVOLVEMENT

Starting to sort out priorities

On a sheet of paper for each small group of two or three, mark out five concentric circles and label each ring: Household, School or Job, Neighbourhood, Nation, World.

Mark out four sections in each circle, and in each write: What it's like, What I/we like best, What change I/we would like to see, What I/we could do to help bring about that change.

Each small group should put one or two phrases in each space, with appropriate discussion.

The ideas are then shared, and a common set of results recorded on a larger group sheet. If the aim is to reach a consensus, it may be better to use this as a way of stimulating discussion and recording progress by concentrating What it's like, What I/we like best, What change I/we would like to see, in one session and What I/we could do to help bring about that change in the next, after reviewing your resources.

He who would do good must do it in minute particulars.

William Blake

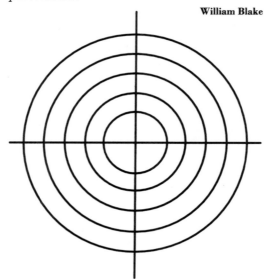

GROUP RESOURCES SURVEY

Each person spends fifteen minutes thinking about the resources s/he has access to, which could be useful in the areas already identified as priorities. List them under the headings: Skills/ knowledge, Time, Equipment, Premises (other categories may occur to you). This could be done by households together before the session.

Share these together in small groups, and try and add new ones—help one another to realize resources you have forgotten.

Then come together as a group and make a Group Resource List. Then add to this another set of resources within the church as a whole, under the same headings. You may be able to use these when it comes to taking action.

One step at a time is enough for me.
                                                    Gandhi

Examples

A caravan in the country may be an ideal way to help unemployed people get away for a short holiday.

A skill with DIY may help insulate an old person's home.

A skill at drawing may be useful in designing posters for fundraising events.

A spare room may be a temporary home for young person just leaving a prison.

An unused garage may be a base for a food co-op.

An ability to communicate may help persuade the council to start a recycling scheme.

A couple of hours a week may get the shopping done for an elderly neighbour.

An organization skill may help start a credit union.

A video might record programmes for use in educating the group about housing issues.

A church building might become the centre for a job-club for those seeking work.

Evenings spent babysitting might be the time to write letters.

When I give food to the poor they call me a saint; when I ask why the poor have no food they call me a communist.
                                                    Helder Camara

HOUSING AND HOMELESSNESS

1

Christians are undoubtedly concerned with housing and homelessness. They need to be. There are at least one million people in Britain today who are homeless in one way or another, and agencies for the homeless (including Christian ones) see the future as increasingly bleak unless action is taken soon.

The definition of homelessness varies of course—from those who are sleeping rough on the streets or in temporary accommodation to those sleeping on other people's floors—but however defined, the homeless have one thing in common: a lack of that 'security, privacy, sufficient space; a place where people can grow, make choices, become whole people' so aptly described by the Church of England's *Faith in the City* report.

In the Gospel according to Matthew, we are reminded of Jesus' concern with the least powerful in society:

'Lord, when was it that we saw you hungry and fed you, or thirsty and gave you drink, a stranger and took you home, or naked and clothed you?'... And the king will answer, 'I tell you this: anything you did for one of my brothers here, however humble, you did for me.'

The necessary nature of our Christian response to the 'stranger'—the homeless—is uncomfortably clear.

'But,' people will say, 'it's more complicated than that.' At one level, yes it is. So much so that some workers in the housing field describe the situation which exists today as one of 'institutionalized sin', where society has chosen to impoverish one section of the community in order to subsidize another.

At the deeper level however, the problem is one of institutionalised sin. Despite the inequity of housing subsidies in general and Mortgage Interest Tax Relief (MITR) in particular, a majority of the population financially benefit from the situation. In this climate neither of the main political parties are prepared to contemplate the abolition of Mortgage Interest Tax Relief with a fairer system of housing subsidies.

Niall Cooper, National Organizer,
Churches National Housing

You were homeless and I gave you my Mortgage Interest Tax Relief? Perhaps.

Any mention of political parties may set warning bells ringing for some Christians, but any change in society is in some sense political (with a small p) and need not be Party Political or divisive—although many Christians will choose to work out their faith in a conventional, political way.

For those of us who are as 'safe as houses' it is hard to imagine the insecurity and stress and sense of worthlessness which being homeless engenders, but understanding the scale of the problem and listening to those who are victims is a start. The good news is that there is a surprising consensus for action amongst those agencies concerned with homelessness and there is something which we can do affect the Big Issue.

HOMELESSNESS TODAY

WHO ARE THE HOMELESS?

When we think of the homeless, the picture that readily springs to mind is that of a 'down and out' sleeping rough on the streets of London. If we are not careful, their plight can simply be dismissed as a drug problem or a drink problem or any other problem which labels the situation as their fault. When in doubt—blame the victim.

The majority of the homeless do not, in fact, sleep rough—though a scandalously large number do so. In September 1991 there were 8,000 people sleeping rough at any one time (around a third on the streets of London); 59,800 were in temporary accommodation (a record high); 168,850 were officially accepted as homeless and 760,000 were described as the hidden homeless (Department of the Environment 1991). A conservative estimate puts the total of those seeking a home but unable to find one as one million; CHAR (the Campaign for the Homeless and Rootless) say that the total could be double that figure.

The 'hidden homeless' include people staying in relatives' homes or sleeping on the floor of friends' houses. In addition, there are thousands of women who are trapped in a violent relationship but who cannot leave for fear of becoming homeless; others are trapped in poverty-line jobs because with it goes 'tied accommodation'.

There are many routes to homelessness; according to CHAS (the Catholic Housing Aid Society) nearly half are made homeless by parents and relatives no longer able to accommodate them, 17 per cent become homeless because of the breakdown of a relationship with a partner, 13 per cent owing to mortgage/rent arrears and 11 per cent owing to loss of private rented accommodation. Many working in the housing agencies would say that the figure for those on the streets represents a serious underestimate.

There are many routes to homelessness: losing a job and being unable to pay the rent or mortgage; breakdown of the family; escape from violence or abuse; being unable to cope—perhaps through mental illness (the recent move to care in the community for mentally ill people has considerably added to this). The safety net which we offer is full of holes and those already on the margins of society are further marginalized.

Single young people are particularly vulnerable. Although we like to imagine that the family is a safe and secure place, we know that an estimated one in ten children suffer from sexual or physical abuse, and this is reflected in homelessness statistics. According to the National Children's Home, approximately 100,000 young people are living on the streets (Shelter put this figure even higher—150,000), of whom 40 per cent have been in care. Even if these young people have dealt with the problems which took them into care, there is very little support when they leave to help them set up in independent living. An increasingly common phenomenon is for young women, on leaving care, to look to replace the lack of love from their childhood by having a child of their own. In London more than a third of all those in temporary accommodation are single mothers.

Other surveys into homelessness confirm this picture of vulnerability; four out of ten women (including young women) have left home because of sexual abuse.

Local authorities have priority criteria for the homeless. In this situation families with children, reasonably, gain first priority but with so little accommodation available (see below), this means that the single homeless fall through the net.

Changes in the benefits system since 1988 have also exacerbated the situation for young people. Those aged between eighteen and twenty-five receive reduced levels of Income Support and Housing Benefit, resulting in many young people being unable to take up any offer of housing. For sixteen and seventeen year olds the situation is worse—they cannot claim benefit at all, except in very restricted circumstances.

Those who are already discriminated against in society are over-represented in homelessness statistics. In the London Borough of Brent, for example, 70 per cent of those who are homeless are black. In Tower Hamlets this rises to 90 per cent (Policy Studies Institute 1987). The London Research Centre estimate that 40 per cent of those accepted as homeless in London are black (the UK has a 7 per cent black and ethnic minority population). Even when accommodation is available, the disadvantaged are further disadvantaged; according to CHAS, 44 per cent of local authority hostels (and other accommodation) have no disabled access.

A TEMPORARY SOLUTION?

When an individual, or family, cannot be housed permanently they are housed in temporary accommodation—often in bed and breakfast hotels. Of the 60,000 accommodated in this way, one fifth live in one room. In London (1989) 7,500 families were housed in this way—a total of 7,000 children (London Research Institute).

Bed and breakfast, in this context, is a long way from the stuff of cosy seaside holidays. In many cases a whole family must live in one room, and the lack of privacy—or even the lack of a lock on the door—is only one problem these families face. A 1988 report (by the London Food Commission, SHAC and Shelter) recorded that 'many of the children had to share

a bed with an adult, and the bedrooms often had no rooms for table and chairs. Most families had to share a WC and bathroom, sometimes with a large number of other people. Half the hotels were estimated to be illegally overcrowded. Hotels were often dirty and conditions unhygienic.'

I feel as if you're in this box, and the box is closed tight, and you can't get out. I just feel, get me out of here, whatever way, just get me out! Half the times I've had to keep the door open, to see who was going past, so I knew that the feeling was only a dream, there are other people in the hotel as well as me.

Deirdre, in *Bed and Breakfast: Women and Homelessness Today*, The Women's Press

In February 1989, the costs of B & B were given (in Hansard) as £14,600 per year per household compared with £8,200 for building or renting a house in the public sector. The cost of B & B to local authorities in 1988/1989 was £95 million in London alone. This may seem a nonsense, but, as things stand (see below), local authorities' hands are tied.

CASTLES IN THE AIR

My home is my castle.

How did we come to this? A number of trends have all acted together to result in the current desperate situation: the decline of the private rented sector; the decline in the number of council houses to rent; the escalation in house prices and economic support for house buying—independent of financial means.

In 1914 seven out of ten people rented their home, in 1974 50 per cent were housed in the public sector but by 1990 only 15 per cent were housed this way.

21

During the 1980s many people sought to gain security by buying their own home—supported by the government, which wanted to see a 'property owning democracy'. Owner occupation increased from nearly 55 per cent in 1979 to 66 per cent in 1989. Amongst these new owners were ex-council tenants who chose to exercise their 'right to buy'.

There was a boom in both ownership and prices. The vastly over-inflated prices meant that many couples had to extend themselves to the limit to afford any house at all. Families frequently depended on two incomes to have any reasonable hope of a mortgage. Those who could not afford to buy (at the new high prices) were left with a rented housing market which had shrunk and whose prices were also on the increase.

Families who bought houses at these inflated prices were particularly vulnerable to recession or shrinkage in the job market. In March 1992 mortgage repossessions reached a record high of 75,540 with over a quarter of a million (275,350) additional families more than six months in arrears in mortgage payments.

The decline of the rented sector over a similar period has also been dramatic. In 1970 there were 131,272 local authority (council) houses under construction. By 1980 this had fallen to 34,493 and a mere 7,518 in 1990. During this period, total subsidy of mortgages cost the government £1,770 million (1989/1990 equivalent) and in 1990/1991 £7,220 million (also standardized to 1989 values for the pound). The capital spending by government on housing reflects this—down from £8.5 billion in 1974 to £1.2 billion in 1988/1989.

This amounts to a change in subsidy, one which has left the poor reeling, and which was noted by the Church of England's *Faith in the City* Report:

The promotion of home ownership is a deliberate political decision, encouraged directly by central government subsidy and indirectly by the withdrawal of subsidy from local authority housing and the pushing-up of rents. The cost of choice for the majority is the absence of choice for the minority who will never be able to buy ... As the Shaftesbury society argues, 'the Right to Buy and the growth of owner-occupation are effectively carried on the backs of poor people'.

The need for rented accommodation has remained and the private sector has not been able to provide rented accommodation at affordable prices. The private rented sector has not expanded. Neither have Housing Associations been able to make up the difference: in 1981 there were 19,000 starts, compared with 15,000 in 1990.

Although we may picture homelessness as an urban, even inner-city, problem, the housing crisis now affects many in rural areas. The provision of affordable homes there is known to be only one tenth of need. The cost of living is higher in rural Britain. In some parts, villages have become dormitory towns for the cities, or rural retreats for second home owners. The inevitable tension here is the effect that such 'in-comers' have on raising housing prices. With fewer jobs in the countryside and housing costs rising, there is an exodus to the towns by people born in the country.

According to surveys by the Association of District Councils and the House Builders Federation, two out of every five new, younger, couples have no choice but to rent. In the view of most of the Housing Charities (including Christian agencies) there will always be a substantial minority whose only option (because they simply do not earn enough) is to rent; to fulfil their needs we need 100,000 units of accommodation built each year. As the situation stands, local authorities lack housing not only for the homeless but for those of the homeless who have been declared a priority.

And what about the money from the sale of council houses? There is up to an estimated £8 billion from such sales on hold. For the most part, councils are restricted from spending this money on building new housing.

As the Catholic Bishops' Conference stated:

In the last analysis, housing is more than economic, it is a matter of humanity and morality, as well as economics.

Housing is a Moral Issue

WHERE DO WE GO FROM HERE?

There is a broad consensus amongst those concerned with homelessness which includes the need for:

◆ More awareness of the problem in our communities. Cathy still hasn't come home.

◆ A review of Mortgage Interest Tax Relief which could release up to £8 billion per year to be spent on affordable housing. Tax relief should be targeted on those with lower incomes. This is not as contentious as it sounds. A MORI poll carried out for Shelter found that 71 per cent of the public favours a more targeted system of tax relief/benefit.

◆ The building of low-cost housing at the rate of 100,000 new homes a year.

◆ Stringent health controls on temporary accommodation and a move to spend the money on permanent homes.

◆ Freeing of the money from past sales of council houses—the capital receipts—in order to build more housing.

◆ Changes in benefit for the young, particularly the restoration of full Income Support and Housing Benefit for eighteen to twenty-five year olds and a review of the provision for sixteen to seventeen year olds.

◆ A co-ordinated housing policy for the UK.

▮ GROUP WORK

Unless you live and worship in the centre of a large city you may be unaware of homeless people. But all Christian communities live amongst the homeless—even if they are 'invisible' to us. A significant part of this section will look at how the homeless can be made more 'visible' to us, and will help us find out how important the idea of home, and the loss of it, is to us.

A SUGGESTED FORMAT

Reading the introduction to this section and 'Homelessness today' may help your group by giving a general background to the issue of housing and homelessness. But this is general, and to understand the situation as it affects your community you will need to do some local research.

'Understanding homelessness' suggests a series of ideas to help you find out more about homelessness and housing in your area and to prioritize your concerns.

'The Bible and homelessness' looks at some of the biblical principles which shape Christian thinking on the issue. 'Thoughts and actions' puts together quotes about homelessness with success stories about how Christians and others are working to alleviate the problem of homelessness. This may act as a prompt to discussion or suggest ideas for your group.

UNDERSTANDING HOMELESSNESS: IDEAS FOR THE GROUP

Facts and feelings

Each person should recall his or her experience of housing: Where have I lived? In what kind of accommodation? Where do I live now—what is it like? What were, and are, the positive and negative experiences? Making notes could be useful.

Each person should then tell his or her story to the group and the experiences should be collated.

At the end of the exercise, the group should be aware of the range of experience it has and what experiences are missing (does anyone have any experience of homelessness—perhaps of being one of the 'hidden homeless' camping out in someone else's house?). If people are self-conscious about their experiences, they might prefer to write them down; the stories should be mixed up so that they cannot be identified with an individual, and the accounts read out.

The end should be the same: what do we associate with happiness and home? What do we know about homelessness? What do we need to find out?

You may like to take this exercise further and explore more explicit feelings about security, privacy, threat or vulnerability. When did they as individuals feel most secure, happy, insecure, cramped or threatened about where they lived? Once again, the aim is to discover what the group feels are the essentials for security, privacy (or any other concepts which come from the discussion). This exercise too can be carried out in written form if people feel more comfortable this way.

Finding out

Because homelessness is often invisible, discovering the extent of the problem in your area is an essential start to both awareness and action. The most practical option will probably be to divide the tasks up between the group, allowing two or three weeks to find out what you need.

◆ Who's in need?

How many people live in hostels in the area? How many are in B & B? How many are on the council waiting list? What is a priority case for the council?

How many houses/flats are there available each year? How many people are refused assistance under the homelessness legislation and why?

The best source of this information will be the local council housing department and/or homeless persons unit (as opposed to the County Council). If you live in a town this will be either a Borough or Metropolitan Authority, in rural areas it will be the District Council.

The council may be able to tell you how many people are sleeping rough—if not, a good source of information is the Salvation Army, who have a fine record of helping the homeless.

Other sources of information are the Citizen's Advice Bureau and local housing associations. Both will be able to tell you about the local situation.

◆ What's available?

You may find it useful to make a housing map of your community—what kinds of housing is available: tower blocks, Victorian terraces, modern council houses (still rented or owned?), large houses. Photographs would be very useful. You could turn this into a creative exercise and make a large display. The housing department may have a map to lend you—they have recently surveyed houses for the new council tax—or try the planning department. Try to visit, or at least walk around, council house estates; try to see some temporary accommodation—B & B or hostels. Obviously, sensitivity is required—these are people's homes.

◆ Costs

Look in the local paper and find out the prices for typical houses in your area, or visit estate agents.

Now look at the average wage. The local employment office will be able give information here—or just go in and look at the average pay for an unskilled worker.

Do the same with benefits. Find out from the local DSS office what the average benefit is for a married man with two children. What kinds of benefits are available if you rent a house or buy?

At the end of the exercise, when you have all the information on hand, try to work out how much someone in your area would have to earn to be able to rent from the council or housing association, or to buy. Is there anything to buy or rent for a family dependent on the wage of an unskilled worker? What proportion of their income would families earning a range of incomes need to spend? Don't forget Mortgage Income Tax Relief when calculating the costs to home owners.

THE BIBLE AND HOMELESSNESS

Leviticus 25. The year of the Jubilee: a radical way of reducing debt and breaking the cycle of poverty. How would we instigate a year of Jubilee in the 1990s? Would anyone vote for it? Can you suggest an alternative?

Psalms 31 and 88. Deal with feelings of despair and isolation. How would we help God to 'work a miracle of unfailing love' for someone in 'sore straits'?

Isaiah 5:8–9; Jeremiah 22:13–17; Micah 2:2, 3:1–4. All these readings deal with the actions of the unjust and God's judgment of them. How should 'shame on the man who builds his house by unjust means' be interpreted today? How would someone who was homeless see this?

Mark 12:38–40. The theme of justice continued; here Jesus points to the hypocrisy of those in authority passing sentence whilst 'eating up the property of widows'.

Luke 4:18–19; Isaiah 61:1–9. Jesus identifies his good news with the message of the prophet Isaiah and makes clear that his salvation is inevitably linked with justice to the poor.

Luke 19:1–10. The story of Zacchaeus and his property. In allowing God to move us to generosity and justice we find salvation.

Matthew 8:18–20; Luke 2:1–7. These quotations indicate realities in the life of Jesus; that he was born in an occupied country with little security. The Gospels recall his life staying with friends, moving on and preaching, but in Matthew 8 we hear a rare note of pain. What does it mean 'to follow' here?

Acts 2:42–47, 4:32–35. These passages describe how the early church dealt with poverty. Can we emulate this today? If not, how close dare we come?

THOUGHTS AND ACTIONS

'Pedigree Chum', 'Bold' and 'Pampers'—
the best in my experience . . .
. . . for healthy bones, strength and keeping dry . . .
. . . That's what you need . . .
. . . for sleeping rough.
'Andrex' isn't bad either—
but what use is softness out in the rain?

. . . better to make it 'Ariel' . . .
and dream of television and home,
'Cadbury's Drinking Chocolate' . . . and warm . . .
gas central heating.
Heating? 'Bacofoil' is best, forget the rest,
snuggle up with the 'Sunday People'
and sleep 'Independent'.

Eleanor Watson

Every Monday night at Lincoln's Inn Fields, five people from a church fellowship feed over one hundred and twenty people on the streets of London. Almost all of the money is found by themselves and they manage to provide a full meal once a week. This is the Lord's Mobile Kitchen and they hope to increase their visits to two or three nights a week.

Homelessness is a subject of definitions. Single homeless people do not have a right to rehousing by local authorities and so become 'hidden homeless', or move onto the streets. Someone who has moved trying to find work runs the risk of being declared 'intentionally homeless'. In which case there is no burden on a local authority to act.

One case we have had this year was a women whose husband was violent towards her so she fled with her four children, and went to stay with relatives. Unfortunately the relatives had a large family of their own and there ended up 13 people in a small terraced house. At first this family was not even accepted as homeless by the Council. We finally got them to change this decision so that the family did get homeless priority.

Church Advice Worker, Leeds

In 1987 Leeds Churches joined together with other agencies to form Nightstop. Volunteer hosts take in a young, homeless person for one or more nights. Each volunteer host has a co-ordinator who takes calls from one of several referral agencies. By July 1991 over four hundred young people had been helped. This is what one user said of Nightstop said: 'I don't think I would be here, where I am now, if Nightstop hadn't been there to help me. I'd have just given up altogether.'

The Diocese of Southwark has persuaded the Charity Commissioners to allow parish-owned land to be leased to the diocesan housing association to provide low-cost housing which can be rented out at affordable prices to those in need.

... the poor have a right to a home, which is not dependent on their ability to pay. This must be our starting point.

Faith in the City

In Blackpool an ecumenical group concerned with housing and other issues formed themselves into the Blackpool Church Action Group on Poverty. They undertook a survey and information-gathering exercise on the plight of the homeless and the availability of housing in their area. Following this, they made a significant impact on local government and succeeded in persuading the council not to cut funding to a charity-run hostel for the single homeless, and encouraged them to set up a local forum on housing.

A Prayer from the Churches National Housing Coalition

Jesus, lover of humanity and brother and sister to us all, help us to find you in those who have no place in our society, who live beyond the pale, who reject themselves because they feel unloved. Give us the hope to overcome the world. Strengthen us and give us freedom and the courage to fight against injustice. Amen

If a brother or sister is ill-clad and in lack of daily food, and one of you says to them, 'Go in peace, be warmed and filled,' without giving them the things needed for the body, what does it profit? So faith by itself, if it has no works, is dead.

James 2:15–17

Read these through individually and discuss the one that particularly struck each of you—why?

ACTION ON HOMELESSNESS

Having worked as a group on the housing and homelessness issue, you may have decided on which aspects of the problem most concern you and know the kind of action you wish to take. This section aims to add ideas to your discussions and to suggest some actions both individually and in the wider community.

ACTION IN THE HOME

Working on homelessness is much easier in a group than on your own; even so, there are things that you can do:

◆ Increasing awareness. Prejudiced attitudes to the homeless are common; being informed (perhaps by doing some of the research listed above) will help you to counter any glib stereotypes. This might occur naturally in conversation or you may feel that you want to respond to something which you have seen on TV or read in the papers.

◆ A more radical approach is to share your home in some way. As we saw in the work of Nightstop, even sharing your home for a very limited period may give someone the breathing space they need. Needs range from the single, young homeless needing an overnight stay to women escaping violence and needing an emergency safe house. Your local volunteer bureau or social services will have lists of organizations which need this support.

◆ Organizations already involved in soup runs or kitchens can always do with help. Your church (or diocese if you have one) may already have a scheme running. If you feel like sharing your Christmas, Crisis and other charities appreciate help at that time of year.

◆ Old furniture is often welcomed by housing projects. Once again, Social Services will know of any agencies of this type in your area.

ACTION IN THE COMMUNITY

The obvious question is, What can my church do? The wider community will, inevitably, be involved.

Making the information known
Having found out about homelessness in your area, the first step is to make your congregation/fellowship aware of the local situation. Use any of the usual channels: parish magazine, notice board and so on. If you have made a map then a small exhibition could be planned.

Involving others
If your group wants to develop or support a project on homelessness, you will need to build support in the congregation. It might be helpful to invite speakers in either from one the housing agencies (see 'Resources') or from a local housing association or tenants' association on a housing estate. If you have a youth group they might like to try sleeping out in a cardboard box (you will need to ensure their safety—a luxury the homeless do not have). You could turn it into a fundraising event for an agency working with the homeless.

Don't neglect the spiritual. You could organize a day of prayer, or make one act of worship centre on homelessness. Charities such as Crisis (Crisis at Christmas) ensure that those who are on the margins at least belong once a year. You could draw attention to this by making the crib scene even more relevant this year and drawing people's attention to the homeless. The collection at one Christmas service could go to a charity for the homeless.

Getting involved with others
Having made contacts with housing groups, you may find that the most practical way forward is to assist them in their work. There is no point in re-inventing the wheel. This involvement may be in providing volunteers for a soup run or kitchen, fundraising for the group or by giving time to serve on their committees, or training as a volunteer adviser.

Using church property

Churches, and church halls, represent a warm and dry place—an enormous resource for the homeless. No one is suggesting that people live in your church hall (although several London churches do now use part of their property in this way) but you may decide to provide a meal a week for those with no home.

If you have a very large hall you could consider setting up a furniture project—recycling unwanted furniture to a good home.

Larger projects

Some churches have decided that they must do something more—either set up an emergency accommodation service (such as Nightstop) or work to provide housing locally. If you have decided that this may be for you, there are several general points to make: learn all you can about the local situation; carry your church with you—keep them informed and involved; don't duplicate the efforts of others, and talk to others working in the field—take it slowly and carefully. The 'Resources' section lists some publications which will help: *Walls and Windows* is a step-by-step approach to building awareness and taking action and *A Beacon of Hope* tells the story of one project and shows how it can be done elsewhere.

NATION/WORLD

Homelessness is a national scandal and no matter how much we set up projects locally there are institutional factors which influence the overall housing market. Inevitably this means that lobbying and influencing decision-makers is the way to achieve change. If you are engaged in finding out about homelessness in your area, you may have compiled information about which your MP is wholly unaware—send it to him or her.

You may have concluded that there needs to be government action on homelessness, in which case writing a letter is still a good way to do something about it. Some churches have taken to direct lobbying of Parliament or councils. All those charities and agencies working for the homeless need our support. Either as individuals or as a church we can contribute to their work. In this respect, we should remember that homelessness is not just a UK problem; many who are displaced by war and famine or who live in shanty towns are found in the Third World. Supporting organizations which deal with refugees and poverty in the third world (see the chapter on Poverty) also helps the homeless.

The word of God in the Bible shows the need for prophecy and social action, the need to keep the Kingdom of God in our eyes and to move constantly towards it. It is not enough to care for the homeless people; the social and political structures that make them homeless must be named as evil and confronted.

Andy Delmege, St Botolph's Project, London

RESOURCES

The organizations below rely on voluntary contributions, so please enclose a large SAE when requesting information.

ORGANIZATIONS

CHAR 5–15 Cromer St, London, WC1H 8LS. Campaigning organization working for the single homeless.

CHAS (The Catholic Housing Aid Society) 189a Old Brompton Rd, London, SW5 0AR. Housing advice, research and education. Serves anyone in need, irrespective of race or religion.

Church Action on Poverty Central Buildings, Oldham St, Manchester, M1 1JT. Information and research into poverty in Britain from a Christian standpoint. Publishes *Windows and Walls*.

Churches' National Housing Coalition Also at Central Buildings, Oldham St, Manchester, M1 1JT.

Shelter 88 Old St, London, EC1V 9HY. The largest national campaigning organization for the homeless. Campaigns, lobbies, publishes research and gives advice to homeless people.

The Refugee Council 3 Bondway, London, SW8 1SJ. Gives practical help to, and campaigns on behalf of, refugees.

MATERIALS

Windows and Walls A step-by-step approach to building awareness in the church about home-lessness. Has Bible studies, group exercises, guides to research and case studies. An essential guide for anyone contemplating a housing project. £4 from Church Action on Poverty.

Housing and Homelessness Information Pack £2 from CHAS (address above). Factsheets on all aspects of housing from a church perspective.

A Beacon of Hope How Emmaus House for the homeless was set up and a step-by-step guide to how you and your church might do the same. Humorous, practical and positive. Also a must for anyone attempting a housing project. Published by CHAS (address above).

Briefing Sheets 'Young and Homeless', 'Women and Homelessness', 'Housing Finance', 'Community Care' and 'Race and Housing', all from Shelter (address above) at 50p each.

Just Housing is a newsletter published by the Churches' National Housing Coalition (address above). Up-dates on church housing initiatives and developments in the field.

City Cries the Urban Mission Magazine. Published by the Evangelical Coalition for Urban Mission. Although it is not specifically geared to housing and homelessness, these are topics that often feature.

Homelessness Quaker Social Action. A practical guide, the subtitle is 'What Can I Do?' Contains research, case studies, addresses. From Friends Meeting House, Quaker Court, Banner Street, London EC1Y 8QQ.

Open the Door Action pack, obtainable from Baptist Union of Great Britain, Baptist House, PO Box 44, 129 Broadway, Didcot, Oxon OX11 8RT.

2 THE ENVIRONMENT

Two thousand years ago a lawyer asked Jesus, 'Who is my neighbour?' and Jesus replied by telling the parable of the Good Samaritan. The story is familiar to all Christians: a traveller en route from one big city to another is robbed, beaten and left for dead, and only the Samaritan goes to his aid. It is not only a tale of compassion but one which extends the concept of 'our neighbour'.

In the last twenty years that wider concept of neighbour has been reinforced by news about our planet. We have literally been able to see our world from out there, a fragile ball of matter, a closed system, spaceship Earth, and the news about it has not been good. We seem to have been on the receiving end of a series of packages with the word 'problem' stencilled on the outside, and as we've begun to unwrap them the contents have been found to be labelled 'disaster'. The pollution plume from the explosion of the Chernobyl nuclear power station demonstrated that environmental catastrophe is no respecter of national boundaries; the impact of global warming is beginning to be understood and is likely to be felt the hardest by those who have contributed to it the least, and satellite pictures of holes in the ozone layer tell their own story. In this global village, we have global neighbours.

The Gospels challenge us still further. Not only are we to love our neighbour, but to love our neighbour as ourselves. We do not have to wrestle too deeply with theology to see that we can hardly say that we love our neighbours if we use them as our dumping ground for inconvenient toxic waste, exploit their resources to vanishing point, pollute their air and water or export industrial processes abroad with standards which would never be tolerated here.

Clearly then, there is a Christian imperative to take action when abuse of the environment affects human life; but what about taking care of the planet for its own sake? It is here that Christians have been severely criticized:

Who is to blame for the crisis we face? First and foremost, I accuse the religious leaders of the world. They have fed mankind with the dangerous myth that humanity is somehow above nature, and that it is our God given right to hold dominion over the earth and subdue it ... they are a disgrace.
Desmond Morris

The word 'dominion' comes from Genesis 1 (the King James version; other translations use the word 'power') and has, regrettably, been taken by some Christian societies to mean the same thing as 'domination'. And Desmond Morris makes a good point. Other religious traditions, from Hinduism to the faiths of the native American Indians, have been more explicit about the need for creation to be respected than has Christianity. But the concept of 'dominion' is not the end of the matter for Christians. In Genesis 2, we see a rather different picture of humanity and creation: 'And God took the man, and put him into the garden of Eden to dress it and to keep it.' This biblical sense of the sacred, of dressing and keeping creation, of stewardship, or holding in trust, has continued to resonate through the ages, from the teachings of St Francis of Assisi to religious communities of the present day. However we read the creation story, whether as an exact account of the creation or as a metaphor for God's creative process, there is one phrase which is repeated over and over again: 'and God saw that it was good'. The next fifty years will be the make or break period for some of the world's key habitats and systems—a last chance to 'see that it is good', for as the dodo knows, being extinct is forever.

THE ISSUES

Looking at enormous issues, such as the environment, can be daunting. But understanding the problem is a long way towards finding a solution, therefore this section will make a whirlwind tour of some key environmental issues.

The phrase 'think globally, act locally' has become the signature of the Green movement across the world, and summarizes well the interconnectedness of all our lives. My CFC aerosol is someone else's hole in the ozone layer, my demand for over-packaged goods is a landfill site next to someone else's home, my one-stop hypermarket is bankruptcy for a dozen local shops. For the sake of clarity, this section divides environmental issues into the global and the national, though real life permits us no such nice distinctions.

But before we become too depressed, we should know that great strides have been made in environmental awareness and in finding answers to some of our ecological problems. These victories have been achieved by individuals and small groups of people who have taken the time to care.

Never doubt that a small group of thoughtful committed citizens can change the world, indeed it's the only thing that ever has.

Margaret Mead (anthropologist)

GLOBAL ISSUES

Global warming—the greenhouse effect
Our planet is surrounded by a blanket of gases which insulate it and without which the earth would be a frozen rock floating in space. The blanket of gases act as a greenhouse—but now the greenhouse is becoming too warm because of an unsustainable loading of global warming gases, some of which will remain active for decades.

During the last hundred years the average surface temperature of the earth has increased by half a degree, which does not very sound much, but there is now a scientific consensus that raising the global temperature by as little as one and a half degrees could raise sea-levels by a metre and a half worldwide. Some scientists believe that unless action is taken, this will occur by the year 2030. For Britain this would result in flooding in many low-lying areas and contamination of fresh water by salt water. East Anglia, for example, will need between five and seven billion pounds spent on flood protection.

Along with increased sea-levels, global warming is likely to affect global weather patterns—unusual weather events such a hurricanes becoming more frequent, for example. For the Third World, changing weather patterns would have a devastating effect. The timing of the monsoon rains (on which most of the Asian sub-continent is dependent for food production) could be disrupted, deserts may increase by up to 20 per cent, and flooding would have a life-threatening impact. A global two metre sea-level rise would result in the loss of 28 per cent of the land in Bangladesh and threaten the lives of over a quarter of the population. Whole island countries, such as the Maldives, could disappear.

A mixture of gases is responsible: carbon dioxide accounts for roughly a half of global warming effects (from burning fossil fuels/ wood for transport, heating and electricity production, with a major contribution coming from the burning of tropical rainforests); methane (from decaying organic matter, landfill sites etc.) is responsible for 18 per cent; CFCs, the same chemicals which cause the erosion of the ozone layer (used in refrigerators, solvents, propellants and blowing agents for polystyrene) 14 per cent; nitrous oxide (from agriculture and the burning of fossil fuels) and surface ozone (from reactions of other pollutants—especially from cars) 6 per cent.

The lion's share of global warming gases are produced by the industrialized world; over three quarters of the world's carbon dioxide, for example, is produced by such nations, while the developing world (where the impact of global warming will be at its worst) is responsible for only 15 per cent.

The responsibility is clearly for the developed (and largely, if nominally, Christian) world to begin to control emissions of greenhouse gases. At the 1992 Rio Summit, western leaders committed themselves to 'freezing' carbon dioxide levels by the year 2000. Many would ask, 'what has been done about it?' The solutions to the problems are available; some involve uncomfortable questions about our lifestyle but others, such as energy conservation and efficiency, merely require a little public and political will.

The ozone layer
Between six and thirty miles above our heads, a tiny percentage of the oxygen in the atmosphere is formed into ozone. This is the ozone layer. The energy to create and destroy ozone comes from ultraviolet light (from the sun) acting on oxygen. In absorbing this ultra-violet energy, the ozone layer acts as a safety mechanism for life on earth. Chemical pollutants, such as chlorine from CFCs (chlorofluorocarbons), accelerate the breakdown of ozone; one atom of chlorine can destroy 20,000 molecules of ozone.

In 1985 scientists noticed that the seasonal 'hole' (really a thinning) over the Antarctic had become as large as the USA (a 50 per cent thinning). Similar thinning has now been seen over the North Pole and, in 1992, ozone levels over Britain were the lowest since records began.

Thinning of the ozone layer allows more ultra-violet to penetrate the atmosphere, causing a range of hazards from skin cancer and cataracts to crop damage. According to the US Environmental Protection Agency, a 20 per cent loss of ozone will result in 600,000 additional skin cancers worldwide and three million more eye cataracts a year. In the Arctic a 30 per cent springtime depletion is expected by the turn of the century. The main culprits are chlorine compounds, such as CFCs, which remain active for up to one hundred years. Consumer pressure has lead to these being phased out in aerosols. The UK has agreed to phase out use and end production of these (and some other related chemicals) by 1995. This may be enough to halt, but not to repair, the damage to the ozone layer—nor does it solve the problem of the disposal of tons of old CFCs in refrigerators and other machinery. The next threat to the ozone layer now comes from a chemical called methyl bromide used to sterilize soil (banned in the USA from 2000 and in the Netherlands today) but still used in the rest of the world.

Tropical rainforests
Tropical rainforests represent the most diverse and species-rich habitat on the earth. More than three quarters of the world's species are found there, in an area covering less than one tenth of

the planet's surface. Some of the most common products on our kitchen shelves originated in the rainforest: rice, tea, coffee, cocoa, bananas, mangoes, cinnamon, cloves and so on. The rainforests are also a living pharmaceutical plant—two rainforest-derived drugs, reserpine (used to control high blood pressure) and an alkaloid from the rosy periwinkle (which increases a child's survival rate from leukaemia from 20 per cent to 90 per cent) are already saving lives.

This astonishing part of creation is disappearing at an alarming rate. According to the United Nations, an area the size of England and Wales is destroyed every year—that's one acre every second and one species every half hour. By the year 1987 over one half of the world's rainforests had been lost.

The rainforest acts as an ecological control mechanism, regulating climate and controlling flooding. As much as one eighth of global warming results from rainforest burning. Following indiscriminate logging in Thailand, flooding took the lives of 450 people and caused more than $400 million of damage.

Reasons for rainforest loss vary from country to country. In South America, clearance for ranching and inappropriate large-scale projects (such as dams—often supported by Western aid packages) are the major causes; in Africa, timber felling and cash crop production; and in Malaysia, timber production.

Although human greed necessarily comes into the story, those countries richest in rainforest are some of the countries suffering most from Third World debt. Rainforests are destroyed to make ends meet. Ten tropical rainforest countries have transferred $25 billion per year to the developed world in debt repayments while at the same time their rate of rainforest destruction has more than doubled.

The loss of the rainforest has gone hand in hand with some of the worst aspects of colonialism, exploitation and genocide. The native peoples have been slaughtered, thought of as sub-human and infected with disease (regrettably, sometimes by those who would

'save their souls'). Since the turn of the century an average of one native tribe of people has been extinguished each year and native peoples are still being threatened today.

Since the general public have been made aware of the connection between rainforest destruction and tropical timber products, the UK has reduced its imports by a third. This is a good example of individual action making a difference in the world but it still leaves Third World countries with the problem of making a reasonable living from their natural resources and of repaying their debt to the rich north. Many environmental organizations and aid agencies see the long-term solution in fairer and better trade, appropriate aid, debt forgiveness and sustainable use of the rainforest.

CLOSER TO HOME

Habitat loss

It is not only in the tropics that habitats are under threat. Since the Second World War Britain has lost 95 per cent of its wildflower meadows, half of its ancient woodlands, 60 per cent of lowland heaths, 50 per cent of fens and wet valleys (with 27 marshland plants on the edge of extinction) and 140,000 miles of hedgerow.

Most of these losses have come about as a result of the introduction of intensive farming methods and the advent of the EC's Common Agricultural Policy. However, this theft of the countryside cannot simply be a matter of 'blaming the farmer'; the farmer merely carries out the wishes of the society in which she or he lives, and it is we who set the subsidies and encourage one method of food production above another.

There are some hopeful, if limited, signs. Within the farming community itself there has been an increased interest in wildlife habitats on farms, and consumers have begun to buy organically produced food (produced without the intensive farming methods, pesticides and fertilizers normally used). Even inner cities are

33

finding green shoots amongst the concrete—
there are now sixty city farms in our towns, so
there is a good chance that there is one near
you—and many rural churches are finding that
their churchyard is one of the few, unsprayed,
wildflower meadow habitats left.

Air and water pollution

Changes in agriculture have also led to changes
in water quality. The nitrates and pesticides
used on our land run off into rivers and streams.
Some of these chemicals end up in our taps,
resulting in approximately four million people
in the UK receiving drinking water which
violates European safety standards.

The wildlife suffer too. Illegal water
pollution incidents doubled from 12,500 in
1981 to 23,000 in 1988. About a third resulted
from industry, a fifth from sewage works and a
fifth from farms. Animals sensitive to water
quality—such as the otter—have seen their
numbers decimated since the 1950s.

Air pollution is a similar story. More than
half our woodlands are feeling the effects of acid
rain (rain which has so much sulphur dioxide
and oxides of nitrogen dissolved in it that it has
become acid) and buildings, such as St Paul's
Cathedral, are being eaten away by the acidity.

When coal or oil is burned, sulphur dioxide
and oxides of nitrogen are given off. Power
stations are responsible for three-quarters of
these sulphurous gases, and cars and other
vehicles responsible for half the oxides of
nitrogen. The good news is that there are ways of
solving this problem if we have the will to do it:
by more responsible use of the car and
increasing public transport, by energy
conservation, by fitting 'gas scrubbers' to our
power stations and by using catalytic converters
in cars. 'Catalyzer' is a much nicer slogan to
have on your boot than GTi.

One area of air pollution where considerable
progress has been made is in lead pollution.
Lead is a neuro-toxin which lowers children's
intelligence and affects their behaviour. Until
the 1980s, all petrol sold in this country
contained lead. Now over half the sales are lead-
free. The campaign to remove lead from petrol
began with a small group of mothers in London
concerned about their children's health, and
became one of Britain's most successful
environmental campaigns.

Energy

How we use and produce energy is crucial to the
environment. Much of the discussion about
energy use centres on the debate about nuclear
power. When Britain's first nuclear generator
came on stream in the 1950s the media heralded
it as providing electricity 'too cheap to meter'.
The reality has been somewhat different. Those
who oppose nuclear power point to accidents
like Chernobyl, the difficulties of being
responsible for nuclear waste for many
thousands of years, and the pollution caused by
the reprocessing of nuclear waste (Sellafield has
made the Irish Sea the most radioactive sea in
the world). Costs (if waste disposal and research
are taken into account) are now known to be
higher than for other energy sources and there is
a history of countries who, having gained
nuclear technology, misuse it to produce
nuclear weapons. Those who support nuclear
power can, of course, legitimately point to the
absence of global warming gases produced by it.

This is certainly an important debate, but we
need to understand that all energy sources have
some environmental costs and the responsible
use of energy is one of the key areas in learning
to safeguard creation with integrity. All our
conventional energy forms will run out in the
relatively near future (coal in 300 years, gas and
oil in 100 years and fuel for nuclear stations in
100 years). We can use that time to fritter away
resources or to develop energy sources which do
not end, such as wave power, hydro-electricity
and wind generation.

In the short term, the best way to a clean
planet is through energy conservation and
efficiency (the most effective answer to global
warming, according to the Department of
Energy). If every house (and church!) replaced
one conventional electric bulb with an energy-
efficient version, one power station (with all its

attendant pollution and waste) would be rendered unnecessary.

Our cars and vehicles consume energy and generate pollution too—it is estimated that by the year 2025 the numbers on our roads will double. But this leads us on to issues of transport policy; do we encourage our governments to support effective public transport with its much lower costs per person/mile?

Waste

We live in a prodigal society. Every house in Britain throws away a tonne of rubbish each year, made up of: 100 bottles and jars, 70 food cans, 90 drinks cans, two trees worth of paper, 100 pounds (45kg) of plastic and 300 pounds (145kg) of food waste. This waste must be put somewhere, usually in landfill sites. Around 1,300 of these sites are at risk of contaminating water sources and a further 1,000 are producing the explosive (and greenhouse) gas methane.

Those concerned with this issue often say that the solution is to bring back the three Rs: recycle, re-use and reduce consumption. Recycling not only saves waste but also saves energy—it takes 95 per cent less energy to make an aluminium can from an old can than to produce a new one from aluminium ore.

And there are some rays of hope on our littered horizon—30 per cent of the paper we use is now recycled compared with only 15 per cent in the 1970s.

Other issues

There are some issues which never fit neatly or easily into categories but which warrant mentioning. Population is one of these. Whenever the environment is debated, someone will, quite reasonably, point to the world's growing population.

The global population is increasing, from 2.5 billion in 1950 to 5.3 billion in 1990 to a projected 10 billion by 2050. Much of that population growth is taking place in the less-developed world. At one time, the conventional response to facts such as these might have been to call for population control. The term

'population control' certainly has a nasty colonialist ring to it and, even if we had the right to tell others how to live their private lives, many aggressive population control programmes have proven counter-productive.

Very often the most successful initiatives are those which understand that, in the developing world, a child represents survival and security for a family and, because of high infant mortality, extra children are seen, understandably, as 'insurance'. In this situation primary health care and female literacy programmes are often the most effective forms of 'contraception'.

Even if the population of the less-developed world does continue to rise, we have to ask ourselves the question 'What does this really mean for the planet?' The simple equation of more people equals more impact is not quite so simple when we look at which human beings make the most impact on the earth. The USA, which has only 5 per cent of the world's population, consumes 25 per cent of the world's resources, and a person in Ethiopia uses 333 times less energy than the average American citizen. The average person in the industrialized world uses 10 times more energy, 15 times more paper and one and a half times more food than the average person in the Third World.

Another area of increasing concern, also outside our usual categories, is that of animal rights. From battery farms to testing products on animals (around three and a half million procedures are carried out on animals in Britain per year) the concept of animals having rights is entering the public conscience. Once again literature from other faiths makes explicit the need to respect other creatures. Islam speaks of 'doing good to beasts as . . . a deed of charity', while Hindu literature advocates 'treating animals . . . like one's own son'. For the Christian the message is more subtly given: the 'day of rest', for instance, was instructed for working animals as well as for humanity. Tell that to the battery hen. One of the challenges which face Christians today is how they should treat other forms of life.

▊ GROUP WORK

So, where to begin? From where we are, of course. Each one of us experiences our environment differently; some of us are city types who wouldn't recognize a bee orchid if it hit us in the face, but who may care about air pollution in the centre of town; others may be able to spot a pied-wagtail at five hundred yards but have no interest in the ozone layer at all. Wherever we start from, the planet can use our help, and God can use our talents; whatever we attempt will make a difference.

Your group may have already identified issues of concern to you; if not, the section 'Looking at the environment' may help. You may decide that you want to hear from those who work closely with the environment, in which case a number of organizations listed in the 'Resources' section should be able to offer advice and/or speakers.

A SUGGESTED FORMAT

It may be useful for group members to read the 'Introduction' and 'Issues' sections before the meeting, so that everyone has a similar basis for discussion. 'Looking at the environment' is a set of ideas which may help you to prioritize areas of concern about the environment. 'The Bible and the environment' looks at what the Bible has to say about the Christian and creation. 'Thinking about the environment' is a set of quotations and facts which can be used to prompt discussion.

LOOKING AT THE ENVIRONMENT

In small groups, mark four concentric rings on a large sheet of paper: our neighbourhood (which includes the church), our town/village, our country and the wider world. Do this twice for each group—so each group has two sets of circles.

On one set of circles note down those things which most concern you about the environment (in its widest sense). On the other set of rings, note down all the things which most please you about the environment. Now come together and decide which concerns and pleasures are most important to the group.

You might like to make this a very open discussion. Many people have very strong, happy, childhood memories associated with the countryside or with a particular place, and many people have a profound sense of God in creation when they walk in a woodland or in the mountains or on city streets on a rainy night. All of these affect how we see, and how we wish to protect, the environment.

Maybe your group has no one with this experience. In which case it might be useful to imagine that you can save only one place or habitat and change one thing which endangers the planet. What would it be?

It might also be useful to bring in a week's newspapers (local and national) to help focus some of your ideas.

THE BIBLE AND THE ENVIRONMENT

We have already noted that the Bible is not always explicit about care for the planet, but that does not mean that God's purpose and intention for creation is not implicit in the text. **Genesis 1:9–19, 20–31; Genesis 2:15–18.** How do these stories differ in their view of humanity's place in creation? What do they say about God's view of his creation? Does 'power' or 'dominion' imply that man should have such power or is it a warning that one day man will? In Genesis 2 two words are used: 'abhadh' (to serve, to care for) and 'shamar' (to preserve or cherish). Both imply respect for a gift—not exploitation. **Leviticus 21:23–25 and 19:9–10; Exodus 23:11.** Do these injunctions have anything to say today about how much we try to make the earth yield? **Isaiah 32:15–17.** The wilderness shall become fertile, but only when justice reigns. How does this tie in with the concept of 'shalom'? What does this mean for the developed world's relationship with the less-developed world? **Psalm 137.** 'The rivers of Babylon' was probably a marshy area outside the city, unfit for building and carrying waterborne disease. How does someone 'sing the Lord's song' in the inner city or areas of gross pollution like Katowice in Poland?

Psalm 104. A great lyrical psalm celebrating creation. What images would you choose if you were to compose or sing a new psalm? (See also **Ecclesiasticus 43** if you have a Bible with the Apocrypha). What do verses 31–35 indicate about countering the spirit of destruction? **Luke 12:15–22.** If we are not measured by how much we own, what is the measure of our worth? If we want to be at peace with ourselves and the planet, what values should we adopt? What are the twentieth-century equivalents of the 'bigger storehouses'? Are we impressed by wealth? **Matthew 7:24–29.** A house built on sand: if we are to respond to the needs of the planet what are to be our to be our actions? **Matthew 8:20; 10:29–31.** These remind us that, as a teacher who walked the land of Judea, Jesus was familiar with all the life around him. Everywhere in the Gospels we find Christ teaching parables, using images which people would understand and recognize, such as the fruitful tree, the mustard seed and the lilies of the field. **Romans 8:18–23.** The concept of the 'groaning universe'; the idea that its physical liberation and our spiritual liberation are inexorably linked. **Revelation 21:1–4.** A gift—or something we strive towards here and now?

THINKING ABOUT THE ENVIRONMENT

The integrity of creation

All of creation God gives to humankind to use. If this privilege is misused, God's justice permits creation to punish humanity.

Abbess Hildegarde of Bingen

The world and all that are in it belong to the Lord. The earth and all who are on it are his.

Psalm 24:1

As I looked down I saw huge forests extending across several borders, and I watched the extent of one ocean touch the shores of separate continents. Two words leap to mind as I look down on all this. Commonality and dependence. We are one world.

John David Bartoe, astronaut

The seedbed of ecological destruction is the global division between rich and poor.

Ben Jackson, *Poverty and the Planet*

The Spirit and creation

The earth dries up and withers, the whole world withers and grows sick; the earth's high places sicken, and the earth itself is desecrated by the feet of those who live in it.

Isaiah 24:4–6

Teach your children what we have taught our children, that the earth is our mother. Whatever befalls the earth befalls the children of the earth. If we spit upon the ground, we spit upon ourselves. This we know. The earth does not belong to us; we belong to the earth ...One thing we know, which the white man may one day discover—our God is the same God. You may think now that you own him as you wish to own our land; but you cannot. He is the God of all people, and his compassion is equal for all. The earth is precious to God and to harm the earth is to heap contempt upon the Creator.

Chief Seattle of the Suquamish Nation

One of the most crucial tasks for Christians today is therefore to reinterpret the meaning of 'dominion' in terms of stewardship and ecological responsibility for life on Earth. But it is only the beginning, for it must be acknowledged that the established Churches have got themselves into frightful pickle ... It seems to me so obvious that without some huge ground swell of spiritual concern the transition to a more sustainable way of life remains utterly improbable.

Jonathon Porritt, Seeing Green

We have invented an eighth deadly sin ... Never before has it been possible for one generation to do so much damage in such a permanent and profound way. The present time—just these few decades in which we have been fated to live our lives—is the most crucial time ever for life on this planet. We hold the future of all life in our hand, indeed, we must decide if there shall be a future.

John Seymour & Herbert Girardet, Blueprint for a Green Planet

Global issues

It is time to stop waffling ... and say that the evidence is pretty strong that the greenhouse effect is here.

Dr Jim Hansen, US scientist, NASA

The American lifestyle is not up for negotiation.

President Bush, before the 1992 Rio Summit

Fact: an average person produces between one and two kilograms of carbon dioxide a day. A car produces that much in ten minutes.

We have not inherited the earth from our fathers, we are borrowing it from our children.

Lester Brown, US environmentalist

It's as though the nations of the world decided to burn their libraries without bothering to see what is in them.

David Jansen, University of Pennsylvania, on the loss of the rainforests

Water and air

Praised be my Lord for Sister Water, which is greatly helpful and humble and precious and pure.

St Francis of Assisi

If human civilisation is going to invade the waters of the earth, then let it be the first of all to carry a message of respect—respect for all life.

Jacques Cousteau

Fact: a quarter of Britain's sewage is dumped in the North Sea.

Death valley: Cubatao in Brazil has been christened 'death valley'. In the name of progress, industry came to the area and operated with very few pollution controls. Children were often hospitalized two or three times a week; 30 per cent of deaths were due to respiratory disease and the main cause of death was cancer of the lung. With the help of the local priest a campaign was set up to draw attention to the valley: 'My work consists of getting people to come to meetings and explaining the health risks they are facing. I tell them that if they act together they can be more powerful and can bring about change locally.' The campaign has had some success. Since the late 1980s fish have begun to return to the river. However the state owned steel mill can still not afford pollution control—the first priority for the Brazilian government is debt repayment.

You know that the air and water are being polluted, as is everything we touch and live with, and we go on corrupting the nature that we need. We don't realise that we have a commitment to God to care for nature.

Archbishop Oscar Romero

Habitat and wildlife

Until he extends the circle of his compassion to all living things, man will not himself find peace.

Albert Schweitzer

Even if there is only one tree full of flowers and fruits in a village, that place becomes worthy of worship and respect.

The Mahabharata

Fact: at the end of the war there were over one million agricultural workers in Britain. There are now around a quarter that number.

Small victories: Whales are some of the most beautiful and intelligent of mammals. At the height of commercial whaling, around 40,000 animals were slaughtered each year. By 1985, public pressure had effectively put an end to whaling—although Japan and Norway still campaign to do so. In 1982 the Wildlife and Countryside Act made trading in endangered species illegal.

Before them the land is a garden of Eden, behind them a wasted wilderness.

Joel 2:3

*We spray the fields and scatter
The poison on the ground
So that no wicked flowers
Upon our farm be found.*

Sir John Betjeman

Fact: more than a million people worldwide are estimated to suffer from pesticide poisoning each year.

Waste, demand and the small matter of lifestyle...

There is enough for every man's need but not for every man's greed.

Mahatma Gandhi

Live more simply, that others may simply live.

Motto of the Christian Lifestyle movement

Fact: in the past twenty years, the volume of packaging in Britain has trebled.

The world is threatened by growing population, but it is also, even perhaps to a greater extent, threatened by the exploding appetites of the already rich.

Maurice Strong

I resent the creation of a world in which beauty is a reminder of what we're losing, rather than a celebration of what we've got.

Ben Elton, comedian

If a free society cannot help the many who are poor, it cannot save the few who are rich.

President John F. Kennedy

Fact: if the world recycled half of its paper, 20 million acres of forest would be saved for the future.

There are two ways to get enough. One is to continue to accumulate more and more. The other is to desire less.

G.K. Chesterton

The environment is not a luxury, nor can it be postponed until later.

President Gro Harlem Brundtland

When I see an adult on a bicycle, I have hope for the human race.

H.G. Wells

ACTION ON THE ENVIRONMENT

GENERAL POINTS

'Only connect!' said the novelist E.M. Forster as a plea for understanding and action. The trouble with the environment and 'interconnectedness' is that it sometimes leaves us with the feeling that because we cannot make a start everywhere, we cannot make a start anywhere. Nothing could be further from the truth—every small step makes a difference. In fact, there are so many things that we can do in our homes, in our churches and in our communities that the ideas for action which follow represent, at best, edited highlights.

One general word. Don't forget to enjoy creation. No guilt, no feeling that 'you should be doing something useful'—just enjoy. Notice what's in bloom or ready to be harvested or planted; make a part of the river or park your own and find out about it; go and see what your local wildlife trust is doing; take a good look at the contents of the sea or beach—get to know it. Why? Because we tend to love, protect and take action about those things which we know and, once we begin to care for one part of the planet, the rest often follows.

ACTION IN THE HOME

Where better to start 'thinking globally and acting locally'? This is as local as it gets.

Do an environmental house audit in order to find out:

◆ what happens to the waste?

◆ how much do we recycle?

◆ how insulated is the house?

◆ are our appliances energy efficient?

◆ what about the products we buy; do they cause pollution?

◆ is our garden wildlife friendly?

◆ are the products we buy tested on animals? Is it necessary?

You can adapt some of the materials listed in the 'Resources' section to help with the audit. The more specific ideas which follow are essential parts of any audit. You can, of course, treat them as a menu of options to choose from.

Waste not, want not

Around 90 per cent of our rubbish goes into landfill sites and more than 70 per cent of what we put in our dustbins could be recycled.

◆ If you are a keen gardener start a compost heap. If you're not, or have no garden, you could always find out if the children know others with furry friends who could use your greens . . .

◆ Recycle—but make it easy on yourself. Most recycling schemes (including 'official' ones) fail to do so because the arrangements for sorting and collecting are not easy to use. The simplest method is to have several boxes (stacking ones are useful) so that recycling takes as little effort as dumping.

◆ Re-use everything from carrier bags to yoghurt pots. Try to make the whole process fun—especially for children; they will invent some amazing ideas if encouraged . . . Try having a 'charities box' at hand for unwanted gifts or clothes.

◆ Try to buy recycled paper products and encourage your shops to stock them.

◆ Think carefully about using disposables.

Wildlife

Our gardens now represent an important wildlife habitat for many animals; they act as oases and 'green corridors' across a hostile landscape. Many species, such as the urban fox, are now as familiar in towns as in the countryside.

◆ Make yours a wildlife garden. Try not to use pesticides or artificial fertilizers. Plant species which encourage helpful insects (bees love anything with lots of tiny flowers). Try to have a small pond or dark, damp spot to encourage frogs and toads. There are some very good books available on wildlife gardening (see 'Resources').

◆ If you don't have a garden, why not sponsor someone else to plant a tree—or perhaps think about an allotment?

◆ Only buy tropical hardwoods if they have been sustainably produced. If the supplier cannot guarantee this—don't buy.

◆ Think about having 'green' family outings.

Energy

The planet and our pockets both benefit from conserving energy.

◆ Begin switching to low energy light bulbs; they use a quarter of the electricity and last eight times longer. They are more expensive at first, but save money in the long term.

◆ Insulate. Draught-proofing doors and windows and insulating the loft space are the best value for money.

◆ When you buy your next appliance try to opt for an energy efficient one. Items such as washing machines and fridges vary widely in how much energy they use.

◆ Use public transport or cycle where you can; clearly this is a limited option in rural areas or for the disabled. Think of the car as a thing to share with others.

◆ Remember to turn off equipment and lights when not in use.

Pollution

The phosphates from our washing powders contribute to the suffocation of life in our rivers, so swapping to low phosphate 'green' products is useful. Similarly, chlorine bleach is a problem for rivers, so swapping to a hydrogen peroxide based one is a good idea. Many 'old fashioned' products such as washing soda have a lower impact than newer products.

Ensure that your car (if you have one) is lead-free and consider a three-way catalytic converter.

Not everyone can afford to switch to green products (though some are actually cheaper). If you can't, or if they are not available, simply try to use the minimum of your normal product.

A consuming passion

Advertising and society at large seem to tell us that having (and buying) more and more will make us happier and more fulfilled—which we know to be untrue; and yet it is easy for that assumption to corrode our deeper sense of values. No one suggests that Christians should be life denying—the very opposite is true— rather 'have life, and have it abundantly', but that abundance should not be at the cost of others. We should be sure that our sense of worth and value is based in relationships.

So try to ask some simple environmental questions when buying a product: Why do I want it? Is there a cleaner or more efficient choice? Were the people who made it exploited? Did the product come from a sustainable source? If those questions can be answered satisfactorily then buy—and enjoy.

A power house

◆ You may want to consider supporting an environmental or conservation group. Without such support, many of the positive changes of recent years could not have taken place.

◆ The pen has been described as the most 'potent anti-pollution device known'. Don't forget that your views count, and that writing a letter—you or your children—will make people sit up and think.

IN THE COMMUNITY

This is a case of not only, but also. All of the ideas above can implemented in the church or workplace (if you work outside the home).

The green audit

Many companies now undertake a green audit and there is advice from a range of environmental organizations (see 'Resources') on how to carry one out. A special pack for churches is available. Essentially, the same questions as the domestic audit apply, with some additions:

◆ Disposables. Greater use of these is made by companies and churches than in the home: everything from towels to tea cups.

◆ Buying policy and recycling. In business, these benefit from gaining support at the senior management level and from researching a list of 'green products'. In recent years, for example, recycled papers have improved dramatically and high quality papers which can take high resolution colour printing are now on offer. Similarly, many photocopiers and laser printers are now CFC free.

◆ Toxic products. In the course of work there are many products used which are hazardous. Since 1989, legislation has been in place which enables employees and unions to gain more information, and greater protection, when working with any chemical. There is also advice available on less hazardous alternatives—see 'Resources'.

◆ Energy conservation simply makes financial sense. In addition, companies can offer company bicycles, bicycle security and racks and car-pool arrangements. Churches should be sensitive about making the assumption that 'everyone has a car' and can attend easily.

Adopting a space

A group of people acting together on one project has great potential. In cities there are tracts of land which would benefit from greening (these neighbourhood gardens have been one of the great urban success stories of New York). In parks the usual 'green concrete' can be turned into a wildlife haven and pollution hot-spots can be cleaned up.

Some of the ideas in the 'Group work' section will be useful here—bringing in outside groups or expertise, looking at newspapers and so on. The goals of the group will probably take some time to evolve and will usually start with a fact-finding stage.

The school

Any audit on the home or business can be carried out in a school—although purchasing policies will differ, depending on how the school is controlled. Environmental education at most schools is excellent and children often lead parents in this! Through parent governors and through parent-teacher associations you can discover what your child is learning about the environment. Is she or he learning about some of the solutions as well as the problems? Are the problems only explained from the developed countries' point of view?

Celebration and worship

Most churches will celebrate a harvest festival, or its equivalent, in the year. This offers an opportunity for celebrating God's work in creation—a number of resources are available to support this. Stewardship is also a common theme for at least one Sunday in the year. With the pressing needs of many churches, the definition of stewardship is often restricted to matters of church finance, the repairs to the roof or the church heating system, but there is scope for a much wider definition which includes the concept of being 'wise stewards of creation'.

THE NATION AND THE WORLD

Any positive action which you have taken in your home, your school, your workplace or your community will already have made a positive difference to the world. But what next? Some global problems require national and international action. There are two main ways of helping:

◆ Writing letters. Very old-hat, very common—very effective. MPs and MEPs and companies do take letters seriously—especially when they are from an unexpected quarter, such as a young person or a church.

◆ Supporting organizations working or campaigning for change. There is a very wide range to choose from—see the 'Resources' section for further details.

▦ RESOURCES

ORGANIZATIONS

The majority of the organizations below rely on membership and voluntary contributions for continuing their work, and therefore an SAE would be appreciated when writing to them. Most produce some free leaflets but if you want more detailed information, ask for a publications list.

Friends of the Earth UK Campaigns on national and international issues including: tropical rainforest, global warming, water and air pollution, waste and recycling, energy, countryside and wildlife issues. Campaigning local groups. Extensive briefings available from the information department (publications list available). 26–28 Underwood St, London, N1 7JQ.

Council for the Protection of Rural England (CPRE) Works on UK-based issues relating to the countryside, wildlife and habitats, rural development and planning issues. Publishes *Campaigners' Guide to Local Plans*. County branches. Warwick House, 25 Buckingham Palace Rd, London, SW1W 0PP.

Greenpeace Involved in non-violent direct action and hard-hitting campaigns on a variety of issues including nuclear disarmament and nuclear power, toxic wastes, marine environments in general and the Antarctic. Greenpeace House, Cannonbury Villas, Islington, London, N1 2PN.

World Wide Fund for Nature (WWF)
Specializes in international species protection and global environmental issues. Extensive educational materials. Panda House, Weyside Park, Godalming, Surrey, GU17 1XR.

Christian Ecology Link An organization of Christians who are concerned about the environment. Produces a newsletter and a useful pack: *Christians and the Planet*, which contains work sheets, discussion ideas, briefings and how to organize a church audit. CEL, 20 Carlton Rd, Harrogate, N. Yorks, HG2 8DD.

Royal Society for Nature Conservation is the umbrella organization for a network of county wildlife trusts and urban wildlife groups. Extensive wildlife conservation projects and reserves open to the public. Practical volunteer projects, works on increasing access (including disabled access) to the countryside. Runs a Watch scheme for young members: practical activities and environmental action. The Green, Witham Park, Waterside South, Lincoln, LN5 7JR.

British Trust for Conservation Volunteers aims to involve people in practical conservation projects in towns, cities and the countryside. Organizes day, weekend and longer projects. Local groups across the country. 36 St Mary's St, Wallingford, Oxon, OX10 0EU.

Health and Safety Executive Advice on all aspects of chemicals at work—including pollution from chemicals and noise. Workplace advisers and inspectors. Baynard's House, 1 Chepstow Place, Westbourne Grove, London, W2 4TF.

Henry Doubleday Research Association (HDRA) Researches into organic methods of growing crops and flowers, preservation of old varieties, links between developing countries and environment. The National Organic Gardening Centre at Ryton-on-Dunsmore is open to visitors and demonstrates organic growing in practice. National Centre for Organic Gardening (HDRA), Ryton-on-Dunsmore, Coventry, CV8 3LG.

Common Ground Encourages people to value their local environment from creative endeavours such as making parish maps (showing what's important in the area), using a variety of methods (collage, montage, photographs), to beating their parish boundaries or parish walks with local planners. Publishes *Holding Your Ground*, £8.95—an excellent guide to local conservation. 45 Shelton St, London, WC2H 9HJ.

Waste Watch is an initiative by the National Council for Voluntary Organizations. Publishes a wide range of materials (including information for schools) on practical recycling. *Recycling: A Practical Guide for Local Groups*, £3.50, and a *National Directory of Recycling Information*, £8.95. 68 Grafton Way, London, SW1W 9SS.

Neighbourhood Energy Action Advice on practical energy efficiency and how to run an energy efficiency project. NEA, 2nd Floor, 2–4 Bigg Market, Newcastle upon Tyne, NE1 1UW.

London Hazards Centre Information on toxic chemicals, less hazardous alternatives and use of chemicals at work. 3rd Floor, Headland House, 308 Gray's Inn Rd, London, WC1X 8DS

MATERIALS

Christians and the Planet: How Green is Our Church? Published by Christian Ecology Link (see page 44 for address).

Floods and Rainbows A study guide on the environment in eight sessions, each consisting of group activity, Bible study and ideas for worship. Published by: The Methodist Church, Division of Social Responsibility, 1 Central Buildings, Westminster, London, SW1H 9NH.

Poverty and the Planet by Ben Jackson, World Development Movement. The relationship between the less developed world and environmental decay explained. Penguin.

Wildlife Gardening by Chris Baines.

Blue Peter Green Guide An excellent book for children and teenagers. BBC Publications.

The Church and Conservation Project Publishes materials on making the churchyard a green place. Arthur Rank Centre, National Agricultural Centre, Stoneleigh, Kenilworth, CV8 2LZ.

Christian Impact Study on Green Issues Information leaflets, Bible study material, ideas for action. Good section on the 'New Age Movement'. Christian Impact Publications, 75 Maid Marian Way, Nottingham, NG1 6AE.

Blueprint for a Green Planet by John Seymour and Herbert Girardet. A practical guide to action. Published by Dorling Kindersley.

3 POVERTY

How then are we to respond today to the plight of Africa where 30 million people are on the verge of starvation? This happens in a world where there is more than enough food produced for every man, woman and child to enjoy three full meals every day with plenty to spare. Despite this, 750 million people at the very least will lie hungry in their beds tonight. But, set this against the fact that last year, unbelievably, 1.3 million tonnes of food was destroyed in Europe. There is surely a moral imperative to bring sanity to this crazy and deadly situation, to restore human dignity, to promote development and the possibility of peace. We must look at ourselves and our lifestyles. We must examine and change the processes and structures of the world which at present promote division and ultimately bring death. We must turn them into mechanisms of international collaboration and human solidarity, and ultimately into sources of life.

Cardinal Basil Hume

Poverty and the people who experience its debilitating effects are in many ways central to the Bible and to the life of Christ, yet they are seldom the subject of sermons, Bible studies or indeed activity in the church that seeks to be the model of the kingdom Christ came to establish; the kingdom that is to be good news for the poor.

Of all the crises facing the world, none is so clear as that facing Africa. Yet poverty, which is at the centre of this stage, is not confined to that continent, nor is it measurable only in terms of food. And its causes and cures are not always so undisputed; like most issues, closer to home means greater controversy.

WHAT IS POVERTY?

When the post-Christmas credit card bills land on the doormat, we might feel we get a personal insight into poverty. Yet we know that temporary debt (or overspending) is a world away from being really poor. And moreover, when we stop to think of the birth, life and example of Jesus, we may experience a twinge of guilt at thinking ourselves poor at all. Poverty is, perhaps, a relative term, and no matter how much we possess, we will always feel poor. In our consumer society this is indeed a real concern as we trample on the earth in pursuit of the unattainable, but even in the UK relative poverty has a real meaning.

We are accustomed, almost to the point of familiarity, with the poverty of those in the world's poorest countries. The images we are given are all too often of people on the edge of existence, driven by war and famine to refugee centres where they die in view of the cameras. What we seldom see are the millions still struggling against the odds—or those now refugees who two or three years ago were still making a go of things. Of the three and a half billion people in the third world, 40 per cent live in what can be termed absolute poverty. They lack the minimum needed to buy the clothing, food and shelter to maintain physical health; around half of these—800 million people, mainly women and children—will be malnourished.

This kind of poverty is a vicious circle. Farmers struggling to make ends meet will not have the resources to cope with a bad year, and will instead borrow money or sell some land. Whatever the crop next year, it will be reduced by the high interest payments or lack of land. Poor farmers will not be able to afford irrigation, or fertilizer to increase production. At harvest time they must sell straight away, rather than wait for prices to rise. Their children are unlikely to go to school. Unable to afford medication, or the trip to a doctor, their children's development will be stunted by illness as well as inadequate food. A few bad years will see them losing their lands and becoming landless labourers working on a daily basis for wages never enough to break out of poverty, or joining the ever-growing army of shanty town dwellers seeking work in the cities.

At the sharp end of this process of impoverishment are those in one of the modern forms of slavery. Children, sold by their parents, hoping for a better life for them, are forced to work in factories—or even brothels—for just their food. Labourers, taking loans from their employers to buy tools, are bonded to work for a wage which ensures they can never pay the debt off. Refugees, fearful of repatriation and not knowing local languages or systems, work as slaves even in so-called developed countries.

While development and the huge expansion of the world's economy this century have created wealth in rich and poor countries alike, they have not eradicated poverty. Indeed, as the gap between rich and poor has grown, the increasing population of the world has ensured increasing numbers of poor people. According to the Swedish government, per capita incomes in sub-Saharan Africa fell by almost 25 per cent during the 1980s. In the same period

investments fell by almost 50 per cent and are now in per capita terms lower than they were in the mid 1960s. Imports in 1988 were only 6 per cent of those in 1970, in per capita terms—a measure of falling incomes, since the value of exports fell by 45 per cent in the 1980s. The debt owed by these countries grew from $10bn in 1972 to a staggering $130bn in 1987, despite repayments being made. Small wonder that the proportion of children starting school is beginning to decline and in some places infant mortality is increasing again.

Compared to these figures, what is there to worry about in countries such as the UK, which have benefited from the growing world economy? A few more statistics: 3 million homes suffer from condensation and mould growth; 6 million families cannot afford to pay for adequate heating; 1 million elderly people are at risk from hypothermia and many thousands more die each winter than do in colder countries. In 1990/1991 nearly half a million social fund loan applications were turned down—nearly 23,000 because they were too poor to repay the loan. The poorest 20 per cent of the population earned a smaller proportion of manual wages in 1986 than in 1886. A 1989 survey concluded that 70,000 single people in London alone were homeless and did not appear on official statistics. More than 50,000 families are in temporary accommodation, often of poor quality. Over 2.5 million people are unemployed and not on training schemes.

The kind of poverty that these figures suggest is different from that we see on our television screens on Red Nose Day or in Christian Aid or Tear Fund literature, but how different? There are two approaches to measuring poverty; one refers to a subsistence standard—the minimum required for physical efficiency. This is a measure one might use in the context of famine. But most people recognize that to be human implies more than merely keeping body and soul together; we have psychological, social and spiritual needs too. So it is normal to define poverty in terms of a

'citizenship standard', below which there is
'...a standard of living so low that it excludes
and isolates people from the rest of the
community'. To be reasonably warm, to retain
self-respect, to maintain relationships and
membership of churches, to live in such a way
that officials and professionals treat you with
respect all require money and resources beyond
the physical minimum. Relative poverty is not
merely a way of excusing want creation.

Poverty in the UK is commonly defined in
terms of people's estimates of what things are
necessary for a normal life. For example: self
contained, dry accommodation with indoor
toilet; three meals a day for children; two pairs
of shoes and a warm coat; money for buses;
beds; heating and carpets; fridge and washing
machine; money for special occasions; toys.
Studies of households on low incomes suggest
that there is a poverty threshold at around 30 or
40 per cent above supplementary benefit level.
Below this, this list of basic needs goes
increasingly unmet. Other people define
poverty simply as living on below half the
average income. Perhaps surprisingly, different
measures all tend to suggest that around 10 or 11
million people are living in poverty in the UK.
That is roughly double the number in poverty at
the end of the 1970s.

The poor in the UK are largely invisible, for a
number of reasons. The biggest single category
are the unemployed—over half are poor. Single
parents, the families of sick or disabled people
and pensioners are all commonly poor. That 20
per cent of the poor are in full-time work may be
more of a surprise. In 1987, 44 per cent of the
adult workforce were 'low paid', an increase
from 36 per cent in 1979. In the world as a
whole, the 1980s saw an increasing gap between
rich and poor, even though the income of the
poorest did increase a little.

And, as in the Third World, poverty creates
its own vicious circle. Those with little money
have to borrow at higher rates of interest (1000
per cent is not unknown from door-to-door loan
sharks). They have to buy in smaller quantities
from local shops: both mean higher costs.

Poorer quality clothes and shoes wear out more
quickly. Coin operated fuel supplies are more
expensive. Britain may not have the extremes of
slavery we hear about in poorer countries, but
increasing numbers of people are accepting
part-time, insecure and poorly paid work in the
face of declining state benefits. Wage rates,
particularly among home workers (often single
parents) can almost match Third World
standards.

But the costs of poverty are not merely
financial. Others may be the guilt of a parent
unable to buy children's shoes or even the latest
toy; the marital stress caused by lack of
resources; the loneliness of being unable to go
out; the health costs of inadequate diet, heating
or housing. To these must be added the costs to
the community, in terms of the contribution to
society of unemployed people, the burden on
health and social services, the rising crime rate,
and the divisions and bitterness that undermine
society itself. Poverty is a great evil, in the Third
World or in the UK, absolute or relative.

WHY ARE PEOPLE POOR?

As we've seen, poverty is a self-generating
condition. An economist's aphorism is that
people are poor because they are poor. You have
to go back in history to find the roots of poverty
in the UK as much as in the world as a whole.
While this may seem a little academic, it is
important, to address the question, 'Isn't it their
own fault?', and to identify why so few solutions
seem to work.

The countries we now associate with poverty,
in Asia, Africa and Latin America, were once
homes to great civilizations, while Europeans
were, so to speak, painting themselves with
woad and living in mud huts. The rise of
European civilization, together with the seizure
of colonies, triggered the industrial revolution

in a way that has determined the development of the Third World ever since.

Trade between Britain and the colonies was initially just that—an exchange of goods. Fine Dacca muslin, spices, tobacco and so-forth came north in return for British goods. However, two examples illustrate a more negative side to trade. The development of a lucrative triangular trade between Europe, Africa and the West Indies was one. Here, in order to produce the sugar needed in Europe, slaves were shipped from Africa to the West Indies. The slaves were purchased with manufactures, including guns: in the peak year, 65,000 slaves for 100,000 guns. This trade not only stripped Africa of huge numbers of the able-bodied young, it set in place a slave/landowner agricultural system that still has echoes today. The second development was the shift from global trade to global production. Increasingly, colonies were used as sites to produce raw materials for our industries, and as markets for our manufactures. Indian-made cloth was taxed, even in India, to encourage exports from the growing British textile industry. The countries of the Third World have inherited economies based on producing raw materials, exchanged for manufactured goods. Coffee or cotton, tin or timber, travel north while medicine and machinery go south.

Today, such a role is increasingly difficult to break out of. In efforts to increase incomes (to pay off debts or just pay for development), Third World countries have increased production of raw materials. Often, such moves have been encouraged by the World Bank and other official development experts. Equally often, they have been to the detriment of local food production and local people, who have lost their land to make way for plantations. But, unfortunately, there is a limit to the amount of coffee we can drink, to the amount of raw material our industry can absorb. As a result, far from incomes increasing, they can drop as prices are cut in the resulting competitive market. Over decades, the prices that Third World countries receive for their exports have

dropped further and further behind the costs of their imports.

One obvious response is to move into manufactures; that's where the money is. It is not easy, of course, requiring investment and skills that are in short supply. But further barriers are put in the way of countries adopting this approach. While crops, such as cocoa beans, may be allowed into the EC relatively easily, once they are processed into cocoa powder, or finished chocolate, they are taxed more highly. Fresh pineapples are subject to a 9 per cent tax, for example. But when canned, the tax rises to 32 per cent, and juice attracts a 42 per cent tax. These escalating tariff barriers are to protect our own industries, of course. But they cost the Third World dear—far more than any aid deals we might make.

While tariffs seldom hit the news, a further major block to the eradication of poverty has done quite spectacularly, as it has threatened our own banking system. The investment needed for industrialization has to come from wealthy countries, and massive loans have been made in the past to many Third World countries. Indeed, after the oil price rises of the mid-1970s, when the oil exporters invested their new wealth in Western banks, such loans became easy and cheap to obtain. (The banks could only accept oil money if they re-lent it out.)

But since those heady days, commodity prices have fallen and interest rates shot up by 400 per cent at the worst point. Repayment became impossible, but in efforts to pay, Third World countries increased the production of export crops, cut social spending and the poor (yet again) bore the brunt of the cost. The most indebted countries owe as much as $1,000 for every adult and child. Many countries have paid interest totalling more than the loan and still owe more than they borrowed! Without release from debt, there is really very little hope for improvement.

It sounds like an insurmountable problem. But, in relation to the amount of money the world spends, the whole poverty issue is a tiny blip. The world spends over $1,000,000,000,000 ($1 trillion) per year on the military, for example. By comparison, the global Forest Action Plan would cost $8 bn over five years, the UN Water and Sanitation Decade, $300 bn, and UNICEF's estimate for the amount needed to meet the basic human needs of everyone on earth is $500 bn over ten years. That is in total less than one year's arms spending (*A New World Order*, Paul Ekins). And incidentally, a second year's arms spending would virtually wipe out Third World debt. The weak bargaining position of Third World countries often means that the only thing that they can offer in order to compete is low wages. Poor wages, poor working conditions, inadequate safety and child labour are all inevitable symptoms of underlying poverty. But governments, keen to attract trade, and companies keen to improve profitability, conspire (sometimes quite deliberately) to prevent improvement. Direct repression is frighteningly common, but the effect of laws impeding unions, or even the lack of enforcement of laws to protect workers, can be just as effective.

While the battle for decent working conditions and wages has (despite recent setbacks) been largely won in the UK, the debt crisis and the rise of unemployment paint a similar picture. Even as the long-awaited green shoots of recovery begin to feature in government speeches, unemployment is set to stay around three million during the 1990s. The heady days of the 1970s and 1980s when it seemed we could buy anything if we borrowed enough have yielded a crop of bankruptcies and business failures, and thousands of cripplingly-indebted households.

A small survey of indebted people in 1988 revealed that a major cause of the crisis was the taking out of large loans, and then a sudden change in circumstances. Unemployment, divorce or separation, pregnancy and the sharp rises in interest rates were major problems. To pay off debts people are frequently 'advised' to take out a further loan, and door-to-door sharks can charge as much as 1000 per cent interest. All quite legal. Assuming all surplus income was devoted to repayment, the survey found it would take nearly twenty years on average to clear the debt. Low income groups would take twice as long. Most people surveyed had help from the family, if at all. Only one in 300 had help from a local church.

Poverty in Britain is ameliorated by a social security system which acts as a safety net. But does it? Over the past twenty years, such provisions have been whittled away, partly because they have not kept up with the 'poverty threshold' and partly because it is becoming increasingly problematic to finance a comprehensive system in a climate which has encouraged state withdrawal from many areas of society.

Poor people have also become more liable to pay tax. While a family of four in 1967 would only pay tax if their income reached 64.1 per cent of average earnings, by 1987 they would start to pay at 37.5 per cent. By 1989, people on half average earnings paid 30 per cent more tax than in 1979; those earning twenty times the average paid around half as much as before. Even more striking is that the government 'loses' £37 billion a year. Social security costs £35 billion—the 'moderately prosperous . . . compete powerfully and successfully with the poor for resources.'

There is also what is known as a poverty trap. For people dependent on social security, there are significant penalties attached to earning any money: the various benefits are taken away, or rent and poll tax payments levied, so that for every £1 earned 80p or even £1 is lost—a marginal rate of taxation of 80–100 per cent! For a single person in rented accommodation, after tax, council tax, rent, income support and NI changes, a weekly income of £5 is worth £5; £40 is worth £5; £75 is worth just £10. If you work twenty-four hours a week, you no longer qualify for IS, and actually can actually become worse off, because of council tax, NI and so on. For single people in low-paid jobs, even a forty-hour week can leave them worse off than being unemployed. (And you cannot refuse such a job, or you may lose unemployment benefit for being 'voluntarily unemployed.)

And, as in the Third World, where unfair trade leads to poverty, in the UK the rise of unemployment carries with it the threat of lower wages, as people compete for jobs. The fact that 20 per cent of those below the poverty line are in full-time work is telling.

In fact it would be truer to say that we have a problem of affluence rather than one of poverty.

The question to be asked is not what should we give to the poor, but when we will stop taking from the poor. The poor are not our problem; we are their problem.

Jim Wallis

The values we have espoused in the development of our consumer society are another factor. Part of the current debt problem is a shift from the old idea of saving up for major purchases rather than going into debt. The word 'credit' now means what our grandparents used to call 'debt'. Where personal integrity once related to the ability to save, to wait, to plan, it now relates more to 'credit worthiness'—how much you can borrow. We now value 'having' more than 'being'. The challenge now is to restore contentment as distinct from possession.

The tradition (and techniques) of frugality disappeared in the new wealth of the 1960s. Protecting oneself against the prospect of poverty just didn't seem important. The destruction of slums and a mutually supportive community also took place at this time. Mass unemployment has returned now that the defences are down. Today, people struggle alone.

THE CHURCH AND POVERTY

It has became commonplace through the hard-nosed 1980s to blame the poor for their poverty in one way or another. This is an idea found also in the Bible, especially in Proverbs and Ecclesiastes, the 'court-originated books'. But, far more commonly, the poor are treated with compassion. There are a number of different words we see translated as 'the poor', from the humble and gentle to the oppressed; from the physically weak to those who struggle against circumstances to keep their heads above water. The words rarely mean 'having not enough money'; poverty is defined in terms of relationships with other people.

Early in the Bible, poverty is rarely written about—as a nomadic tribe, the Israelites shared good fortune—but by Exodus 20, beggars appear as the Israelites settled down and people could own (and lose) land. Poverty at this time is seen as the result of unjust social and economic structures, not just 'circumstances'. By Samuel's time, when a hereditary royalty began accumulating private lands and wealth, we first hear of the poor being despised by the rich; and the prophets begin linking poverty to oppression.

The books of Deuteronomy, Leviticus and Exodus are full of rules and regulations, designed not merely to protect the poor, but to prevent the extremes of poverty and wealth that are the cause of so much suffering and social disintegration. Under laws of Sabbath and Jubilee years, unpayable debts were to be forgiven, land lost in times of poverty returned to the owners and even people sold into slavery released. While commonly thought of as impractical in today's more complex world, such laws set us important principles.

'The Bible is never sorry for the poor. It takes their side and pleads their cause. It is sorry for the rich' and 'The prophets do not ask for charity, but justice' are two quotes that capture the essence of the Old Testament view of

51

poverty. Yet the New Testament seems less clear cut, even though Jesus introduced his ministry with a clear reference to Jubilee (Luke 4). Jesus balances the promises of the Old Testament (if you obey my commands, there will be no poor in the land) with a large slice of realism (the poor will always be with you), but still bases his ministry on the poor and reserves criticism for the rich and powerful. But what of the widely-quoted differences between the beatitudes in Luke and Matthew? These are due in part to the Aramaic words for 'poor' having spiritual overtones, as in the Hebrew words of the Old Testament. Luke was showing the need to see horizontal relationships (between people) as inseparable from the vertical one with God. The rich, he says, are sinners because they are rich; the poor are also spiritually poor because they are oppressed. It is difficult for the rich to be spiritually poor! Incidentally, the word for 'oppression' in the New Testament is often translated in our Bibles as 'affliction', 'suffering' or 'tribulation', so it is not obvious that the original meaning included ' . . . at the hands of others'—a term denoting *justice*, rather than *charity*.

So, the common idea that the New Testament is 'weak on poverty' is largely due to our not appreciating the language and culture. But, if concern about poverty is so central to the Bible, why have the churches in general been quiet about it for so long? Basil the Great, one of the early Church Fathers, wrote:

How can I make you realise the misery of the poor? How can I make you understand that your wealth comes from their weeping? When someone steals another's clothes, we call them a thief. Should we not give the same name to one who could clothe the naked and does not? The bread in your cupboard belongs to the hungry . . . the money which you hoard up belongs to the poor.

Such teaching was common for the first few centuries, until the church became close to the establishment, and could no longer afford to offend it. Most damningly, during the worst period of the church, before the reformation, the Franciscan order was threatened with excommunication unless it gave up its teaching on poverty, which was critical of the great wealth of the church. Even today, the issue frequently threatens to divide the church:

Quite frankly, many . . . Latin American believers don't even believe we are Christians. They ask, how could we possibly be Christians when we live lifestyles of such evident greed and self interest while Christians in other parts of the world don't have enough to eat?

Tom Sine

A major problem for the church is that, while Jesus preached the gospel of the kingdom, we have for many years tended to divorce the two: the kingdom is social teaching and mistrusted, and the gospel is emptied of its social content. 'The rich pray for peace, while the poor pray for justice'— yet in the Bible, shalom is the state in which peace is the fruit of justice (Isaiah 32:17).

We must claim, like Paul, to be 'Citizens of no mean city'. We belong to a powerful, affluent society which can, and must, afford the means to a proper life for its poorest people.

Nowadays the rich no longer ask the poor, 'Why are you so poor?' The poor ask the rich with increasing urgency, 'Why are you so rich?' . . . Poverty is no accident; it is determined by the structures of society.

When I give food to the poor they call me a saint; when I ask why the poor have no food, they call me a communist.

Dom Helder Camara

▮ GROUP WORK

If possible, these discussions should involve people who are unemployed or who have experienced unemployment. It would also be helpful to include people who are living on income support, as their experience will help the process. If it is difficult to find such people to join in, a good starting point is to ask why. Can we bring good news to the poor if we cannot involve them in the life of the church?

It is a good idea for someone to review the 'Resources' section and buy material that may assist the group. Also, if you review the 'Action' section beforehand, it will be easier to make the shift from problem to solution as you discuss the material here.

POVERTY AND WEALTH IN THE BIBLE

Again and again in the scriptures, the exploitation and suffering of the poor is directly linked to the substitution of the worship of mammon for the true worship of God.

Jim Wallis

God and the poor
Deuteronomy 15:7–11; 24:14–15, 19–21; Jeremiah 22:15–16. What do these passages indicate about God's attitude towards poor people?

Jesus announces the reason for his visit
Luke 4:18–21, 6:20–26; Matthew 19:21–25; Acts 2:42–44. In what way did Jesus bring good news for the poor? In what way does the church bring good news for the poor today? How is this expressed in your locality?

Recovery from economic failure
Isaiah 58. 'Isaiah insists that the holy response to economic failure is not the ritual invocation of God, as if he were an elemental deity, but a renewed concern for the poor.' How do our modern-day prophets believe society can recover from its economic decline?

Injustice

Poverty doesn't just happen
Amos 5:21–24, 8:4–7; Isaiah 3:13–15, 10:1–4, 58:3–7; Micah 6:6–8. Ordinary people, traders, leaders and even laws are unjust and make worse the plight of the poor. How does God view injustice? How should this influence our response to unjust systems of which we are a part? How does injustice manifest itself today?

Debt

Lending money
Leviticus 25:35–37; Deuteronomy 15:7–8; Luke 6:34–35. Who borrowed money in biblical times and why? Why was it a sin to charge interest? How might this rule apply today for:

◆ A loan to a poor person to buy food?

◆ A business loan to increase production?

◆ A loan to buy a new car?

Forgiveness
Deuteronomy 15:1–2; Matthew 6:9–15; 18:23–34. Why is debt such a good picture of sin? How far should forgiving wrongs apply to forgiving financial debts? The people of Israel were 'brothers' (and sisters). How far are our obligations to the people of Britain the same?

Help for those in debt
Nehemiah 5:1–13. During the rebuilding of the wall of Jerusalem, harvests were poor and people fell into debt, even sold their children into slavery. Nehemiah speaks and acts against this. Why were people powerless to pay their debts? What does Nehemiah do? What could we ask money lenders and high street retailers to do? Lower interest rates to bank rates? Only lend money after a personal interview (as John Lewis do)? Anything else?

The Bible in today's world

◆ Poverty in Israel is frequently put down to the nation's disobedience to God's laws (for example, Deuteronomy 15:4–5). How far is this true of Britain today?

◆ What is, or would be, the nearest thing to the seven-year debt cancellation the government could do to safeguard the poor?

◆ How does the principle of debt cancellation apply to Third World debt?

◆ Should there be some limit to the interest rate people can charge? (Currently there is none, and rates of over 1000 per cent are quite legal.)

◆ How can our church help those in debt or unemployed within the congregation? In other inner city congregations? In the worldwide church? In our local community?

◆ What reasons do we give for not being personally generous? (Going the second mile, giving to those who ask, lending your coat . . .).

POVERTY TODAY

THE COSTS OF UNEMPLOYMENT

The Christians Unemployment Group identify the costs of unemployment:

To the unemployed person and family:
Destruction of self confidence, loneliness, poverty, poor health, marital stress, isolation from society.
To the community:
Loss of income/increased burden on local authority, pressure on medical services and schools, crime and violence, loss of contribution of unemployed people, bitterness and division.

Which of these are properly the concern of the church? How can they be addressed in your area?

THE COSTS OF LIVING

Figures from April 1992 for a 20-year-old unemployed man in a council flat (weekly):

Rent (housing benefit)	£25.00
Water	£3.75
Fuel	£13.00
TV	£5.00
Poll Tax	£1.15
Income support	**£33.60**
Left for food, clothes etc.	£10.70

A part time job at £2/hour for twenty hours would make him 28p a week better off. As a group, define what you would regard as an adequate level of activity and possessions, then try and cost out the necessary expenditure. Some of you could try and live at this level for a month.

THE DEBT TRAP

Watch *The Debt Trap* video, from Familybase.
Research the interest rates on offer in local shops' adverts and on junk mail through the door: What does credit seem to offer?
What do you think of the reality?
How should people respond?

THE CHURCH AND THE POOR

To what extent has the church remained open to all social groups? To what extent does it reveal a gospel defined by the poor? What can be done to address the problem at home? Is charity rather than solidarity (sharing) the motive behind giving? How would this difference be expressed?

POVERTY AND SOCIAL CHANGE

Society has changed since the war, making poverty more of an individual burden than community struggle. How easy is frugality in our society? What has happened to support networks? What has changed since the 1950s? To what extent is poverty the fault of poor people? How could the church respond to this?

How has society's view of debt and borrowing changed? Why is this? How can the church begin to encourage an attitude of contentment rather than dissatisfaction?

THE CHURCH AND THE POOR

... although we cannot do without good institutions in either Church or society the present structures of the church reflect not a liberative gospel, but structures of power and control; we need to ask who it is that the Church serves. ...the message of the Church, by its example as well as in its preaching, is neither good news to those who are poor in body and spirit, nor bad news to the sinful and self-confident.

... the service we offer comes from those associated with the privileged and powerful rather than those who stand with the poor and powerless.

... judgement begins at the house of God.

How would you respond if someone said these words about your local church? They come from the ACUPA report, *Living Faith in the City*.

REFLECT AND DISCUSS:

Unemployment
How would you feel when asked 'what do you do?'
  when you think you're doing nothing useful?
  when you have no daily routine?
  when you collect your benefit?
  when you cannot buy Christmas presents?
  when you are not invited out for a drink?
  when you get turned down for a job?

How do feelings alter after a year?
Discuss: how does unemployment affect:
  older people?
  younger people?
  married people?
  single people?
  disadvantaged people?

Discuss the differences between:
  unemployment and long term unemployment
  unemployed and unwaged
  employment and work
  job creation and wealth creation

Debt
What does being in debt do to people?
  You rob Peter to pay Paul
  You lie awake all night
  You steal money out of your Mrs' purse
  It destroys your family and friendships
  You can't buy a round
  It eats you up inside
  It cuts off your gas and electric
  It makes you hard
  It destroys your hope
  It makes you bitter against God

Why do people get into debt?
  Too much drinking, gambling and smoking
  They don't budget properly
  You get made unemployed
  Your man walks out
  They cut your overtime
  You borrow more to get out of debt
  Credit is too easy
  You want your kids to have the same
  You don't realize how much interest you pay
  You can't say 'no' once they are in the house

What can churches do?
  Turn your kids away because they've got no subs
  Give you broken toys at Christmas
  Invite your kids on expensive outings
  Change the Lord's prayer from 'debts' to 'trespasses'
  Preach that wealth is a sign of God's blessing
  Treat all people with respect
  Replace cold charity with sensitive care

Encourage people to share
Support food co-ops, credit unions, debt counselling services
Lobby for higher benefits, lower maximum interest rates

How do you respond to these words, collected by the Evangelical Coalition for Urban Mission?

QUOTE VOTE

O God, to those who hunger give bread; and to us who have bread give the hunger for justice.
Latin American prayer

We need to become a church for and of poor people if we are to speak without hypocrisy on policy issues.

. . . the idea of citizenship is a shell of hypocrisy if it excludes the poor from the general prosperity.

Poverty is not only about a shortage of money. It is about rights and relationships; about how people are treated and how they regard themselves; about powerlessness, exclusion, and loss of dignity. Yet the lack of an adequate income is at its heart.

. . . the Church is more comfortable with the comfortably off, and . . . poor people are more remarked on during our worship than present at it.

ACTION ON POVERTY

Review the 'Actions' section, perhaps between meetings, and then convene to brainstorm and prioritize the needs your church could/should address.

A survey of needs, as described below, could form part of the preparation for this. A survey of resources from within the church, and available within the community could form part of the follow-up.

Action here must address two areas of poverty: in the Third World, and in the UK. As we saw in the briefing section, there are parallels between the two, and so action focuses on two causes of poverty in both areas: debt and the ability to earn money. Third World debt is a significant cause of poverty, as is personal debt here. Unemployment is the biggest contributory factor to debt and poverty here, as unfair trade is to the Third World. Alongside direct giving, action on these fronts is essential if poverty is ever to be eradicated.

ACTION IN THE HOME

The major way in which we as households engage with poverty is when we go shopping. While the obvious link is the amount we spend on the trappings of consumerism, rather than making available to the poor, there is another, more positive element at work. The section on 'Consumerism' has some ideas relevant to the first issue; here we concentrate on the second.

Debt

Most of us are in debt in one way or another, but a specific area of concern is the ease with which people can get into unmanageable levels of indebtedness. Pressure grew through the 1980s to live beyond our means, and we created a debt-financed false boom which we have subsequently paid for, in terms both of recession and personal debt. It is the ease with which we can get into debt that is of concern—even the encouragement to do so. Credit cards (when *did* debt become 'credit'?) and high street stores are extremely pushy about encouraging a buy-now-pay-later approach, often with little reference to the ability of the borrower to pay. And it is consumer debts of this kind, when they cannot be cleared, which lead borrowers into the hands of loan sharks. Interestingly, some high street retailers who specialize in the pay-later scene get more profit from the credit deal than the sale!

Why not consider refusing to use store cards until the system is properly regulated? Consider asking your retailer what they are doing to control excessive debt—how do they set credit limits? Do they check credit ratings or (better) earnings beforehand? Consider changing your loyalty to a company such as John Lewis, which takes a more responsible attitude towards credit (and is therefore able to charge a lower rate of interest!).

The major banks are involved in Third World debt and, while they have made some moves towards rescheduling or converting debts, many believe they could and should do much more. The World Development Movement have asked us to cut up our credit cards as an indication of concern. You could perhaps swap to an 'affinity card' where a little benefit is given to Oxfam or another Third World charity. Contact WDM to find out the latest position.

Whether we are buying on credit or not, the kind of company we buy from is crucial. As consumers we have voted for safer and more reliable products and more recently for greener ones. Companies respond more to what consumers spend their money on than to what they say. New Consumer collects information on which companies are the best employers, do most to contribute to society, and have made some progress towards good policies in the Third World.

With upwards of £400 billion to spend, UK consumers are a powerful lot, and informed choices can make a huge difference to the quality of employment in the UK and even in the Third World. Perhaps more of your household budget should go to the 'good' companies. See the books, *Shopping for a Better World* and *The Global Consumer*, or contact New Consumer. That aside, there is the need for more people to review seriously their spending and consider more creative uses for their money. Charitable giving is the obvious alternative, and total giving in the UK is extremely low by any rational measure. Organizations such as Church Action With the Unemployed, Church Action on Poverty, or the many charities working with poor people in the UK or the Third World are finding the recession decreasing their funds to tackle increasing problems.

ACTION IN THE CHURCH AND COMMUNITY

These concerns are mirrored in the church, too. The level of giving is continually under review at many churches, and there are competing claims on the resources. But the claims of the poor on the body of Christ are crucial, and the very authenticity of the gospel is compromised if the church does not take its ministry to the poor seriously. But the focus here is on action, not giving, and there is much that can be done.

The Third World

Third World poverty is an area of traditional (if not always effective) church concern, but it does tend to be tacked on as an afterthought. Building an awareness of the world and its needs into worship may be a starting point. This is the one key corporate activity and can (spiritually and psychologically) set the agenda for the rest of church life. Setting aside times in the service for reflection and prayer is helpful in its own right, too. And setting time aside in the church calendar for particularly focused services is useful, too: Harvest, One World Week, Christian Aid Week and so forth. Collections, simple shared meals and even awareness-raising activities can follow, or be part of the worship. The major development agencies publish ideas regularly.

Traidcraft has been around for many years, though is still not a regular feature of many churches. Seen as a way to incorporate many of the issues mentioned here (lending without interest, paying fair prices, sharing the benefits of trade), Traidcraft is central to the church's expression of concern for the poor. How many church members know why there is a Traidcraft stall at the back?

But it is UK poverty that the local church can engage most directly with.

Unemployment

Church Action With the Unemployed is a national organization encouraging local action. It suggests a range of possibilities, from educating the church population about the place of work in life and worship, to setting up local employment initiatives. If you are contemplating any action on unemployment, affiliate with them.

Depending on local needs, the resources of the church, and what other initiatives exist in the area, it might be appropriate to:

◆ **Create jobs:** The church could employ someone to undertake the many caring or administrative roles for the church. It could employ someone specifically to work with unemployed people. It could financially or in other ways support job creation initiatives. It could together with other churches start a local enterprise.

◆ **Support unemployed people:** Grants for long term unemployed people (to buy equipment to help them do what they want while

unemployed). Encouragement and facilities for self help groups of unemployed people.

◆ **Educate**: Raise awareness about needs of unemployed people; start a People and Work Week—give thanks for the paid and unpaid work which contributes to the community; Lent study course.

◆ **Raise funds**: Unemployment Sunday collections or other schemes to support the work of CAWTU.

Some of these ideas are not to be embarked on lightly, but there is a wealth of experience from churches already well down this road.

Preparation for action should involve these stages:

◆ Make contacts with Christians and other people locally concerned about unemployment (including those in local government and agencies).

◆ Find out how to obtain statistics on unemployment—the local authority or Department of Employment Regional Office.

◆ Contact Unemployment Alliance, The Unemployment Unit, Church Action on Poverty, industrial chaplains, church social responsibility officers, church leaders, for help, advice and contacts.

◆ Research the Press, TV and books: produce publications and displays for the churches, the local press etc. to get support. Offer resources to local churches for unemployment Sunday (the Sunday before Ash Wednesday).

◆ Involve unemployed people, listen to their stories and (with permission) use their stories to educate others.

Starting a local enterprise

This may seem the most ambitious initiative, but in the end somebody has to use their resources to offer a service and create employment. Churches have done it. A number of agencies can offer advice and support:

HMSO publish *Community Business: Good Practice in Urban Regeneration*; NCVO have lots of publications; The Neighbourhood Initiatives Foundation have much experience in involving the whole community in the planning; and the Community Development Foundation and the National Federation of Community Organisations are worth contacting too.

Linking Up, a church-based project in Manchester assisting local enterprises, identifies the following strategy:

◆ Research: Find out the needs in the area, so that the enterprise can offer a service.

◆ Aims: Be clear why you are doing the project. What does it aim to achieve?

◆ Objectives: How are you going to achieve it? What are your measurable goals?

◆ Resources: What people are going to run the project, get it off the ground? You'll need a range of financial, administrative and other skills.

◆ Support: Who can you rely on to help from outside?

◆ Business plan: This needs to cover market research, staffing, premises, finance, management, constitution, marketing and evaluation.

Finally, there are several organizations needing voluntary workers which operate at the local level. Some of these make a special point of involving unemployed people. Why not find out if the British Trust for Conservation Volunteers or Waste Watch operate in your area? If so, you could help find volunteers and make your local environment a better place too.

Debt

The Jubilee Centre, better known for its campaign on Sunday Trading, is heavily involved in debt—concern focusing on the impact on family and community life. The Centre has plenty of resources for churches wishing to get involved, from action guides to Bible studies.

The Centre identifies the following ways for churches to take action:

◆ **Informal support for those in debt**
This can take the form of listening and being aware of the problems and being able to give practical advice on who to contact for advice. Offering transport to advice centres and officials, and offering to support official meetings, can be very valuable to people who feel vulnerable and alone.

◆ **A hardship fund for immediate needs**
With the decline in social security funding for short-term needs, there is an increasing need for churches to establish revolving funds which operate according to biblical principles. The money cannot be a loan officially unless the church registers as a lender, but then repayment should not be enforced anyway . . .

◆ **Informal advice**
The Office of Fair Trading leaflet, *Debt—a survival guide*, offers advice here, but many indebted people will need practical help in sorting out a budget, contacting creditors or seeking expert advice when necessary.

◆ **Debt counselling**
Those with legal, financial or counselling skills could become members of a Citizens' Advice Bureau team, with all the support and training that this offers. Local training can be found through Money Advice Centres, CAB or Trading Standards Office. Debt counsellors need a licence from the Office of Fair Trading and insurance cover. Advice from: Bristol Debt Advice Centre—set up by a local church with trained counsellors, etc. PO Box 719, Bristol BS99 1GS.

◆ **Money management training**
Credit Action (the Jubilee Centre) have a course for use in marriage preparation in church, aimed at prevention rather than cure.

◆ **Credit unions**

Another form of prevention is to start a credit union, in which people pool their savings in a financial co-op and can then make loans far more cheaply than banks. Several churches have begun these, and advice can be obtained from: The Revd Dick Bradnum, The Vicarage, 1 Sunny Bank Road, Mixenden, Halifax HX2 8RX. (Tel. 0422 244761)

In many ways credit unions reflect the biblical model, in that:

loans are made within a 'common bond'— that is, to people known to the lenders and loans are made on trust

interest rates are low

there is some degree of concern about the ability to pay

interest charged is not taken by the lender, but shared as a dividend among members

A rather different approach is to set up a loan/ sharing scheme of major items which are infrequently used. Besides saving money for better uses, such schemes also reduce the demand for credit. Sharing anything from lawnmowers to cars and caravans can be quite informal, or the church could facilitate this through some more organized scheme.

The Evangelical Alliance has a helpful booklet, *Devising an Action Project for the Inner City*, a step-by-step guide to marshalling resources and ideas.

ACTION IN THE WORLD

Poverty is a soluble problem. Despite the apparent enormity of the task, there are clearly the resources to solve it, and the fact that those resources are put to other uses is a political and moral issue. Most organizations concerned with poverty in the UK and the third world put resources into public education—to create a climate of opinion in which the right decisions might be taken—and into lobbying governments.

Join the organizations in the 'Resources' section and find from them the current issues of concern. Write to government, local government and to businesses thinking of investing in or withdrawing from the area . . .

▌ RESOURCES

ORGANIZATIONS

Evangelical Alliance Community Initiatives Unit Whitfield House, 186 Kennington Park Rd, London SE11 4BT. Can advise and help find resources for church-based initiatives in the inner city.

Anti-Slavery International 180 Brixton Rd, London SW9 6AT. Campaigns on slavery in its modern forms: forced child labour, bonded labour, forced prostitution, child prostitution, refugee slaves.

Christians Unemployment Group (CHUG) The Revd Raymond Draper, 5 Church Lane, Wickersley, Rotherham, S66 0ES. A federation of groups in South Yorkshire.

National Council of Voluntary Organizations 26 Bedford Square, London WC1B 3HU. Have lots of relevant publications; send a SAE for a list.

Community Development Foundation 60 Highbury Grove, London N5 2AG.

National Federation of Community Organisations 8–9 Upper Street, Islington, London N1 0PQ.

Church Action With the Unemployed 45 Blyth Street, London E2 6LN. Offers specialist advice on help available for local initiatives, and a national network of help. A directory of local project ideas. Launchpad (small) grants for job creating or community benefit projects are available.

Church Action on Poverty Central Buildings, Oldham Street, Manchester M1 1TJ.

Neighbourhood Energy Action 2–4 Bigg Market, Newcastle upon Tyne, NE1 1UW. Works with Help the Aged and Age Concern on the Department of Health's Keep Warm Keep Well campaign and the Winter Warmth line. Initiatives to improve insulation of houses especially in inner city areas and with low-income families.

Neighbourhood Initiatives Foundation Suite 23–25 Horsehay House, Horsehay, Telford TF4 3PY. Specializes in producing materials to enable the whole community to become

involved in planning its future. Publications list available.

National Federation of Credit Unions. 5th Floor, Provincial House, Bradford, BD1 1NP.

Waste Watch (an NCVO initiative) 68 Grafton Way, London W1P 5LE. Recycling 20 million tonnes of rubbish in our dustbins has great potential: environmental, financial, employment and training—recycling can create jobs and help people to acquire skills. Can be linked to unemployed centre/training project.

British Trust for Conservation Volunteers 36 St Mary's Street, Wallingford OX10 0EU. Involving unemployed people, those with disabilities or other marginalized groups. Runs courses for environmental volunteers, conservation working holidays, weekend and midweek conservation projects.

ACTION/DISCUSSION MATERIAL

An extended Bible study from CAWTU looks at work, creativity, unemployment and poverty. Send for a publications list.

Community Business: Good practice in Urban Regenaration is available from HMSO (PO Box 276, London SW8 5DT).

No Mean City—A Methodist View of Poverty and Citizenship, £1 available from Methodist Publishing House, 20 Ivatt Way, Westwood, Peterborough PE3 7PG.

Debt trap action—Familybase Bible studies, and other material, available from the Jubilee Centre, 3 Hooper Street, Cambridge CB1 2NZ.

Hardship Britain: Being Poor in the 1990s £6.95 from CPAG, 1–5 Bath Street, London EC1V 9PY—gives the voices of people in poverty a chance to be heard.

Tear Fund Bible Studies: *Disciples Living in a Broken World*; *Poverty*; *Justice*.

Towards the Recovery of a Lost Bequest, Roger Dowley. Subtitled 'A Layman's notes on the biblical pattern for a just community', this is a useful source book for Bible study. Not an easy read, but almost a commentary on themes of shalom, solidarity and redemption in the Old Testament, brought into fulfilment in the New. From Frontier Youth Trust, 130 City Road, London EC1V 2NJ.

Living Faith in the City—A progress report, by ACUPA, with study guide for group work, published 1990. From Church House Bookshop, Great Smith Street, London SW1P 3BN.

Rich Christians in an Age of Hunger Ronald Sider. Now a classic, but a 1990 update makes it worth reading again. Hodder and Stoughton.

4 WOMEN

St Thomas Aquinas described women as 'misbegotten males' and Martin Luther was moved to say, 'A woman is never truly her own master. God formed her body to belong to a man, to have and to rear children. Let them bear children 'til they die of it, that is what they are for.' With attitudes like this it is no wonder that many women see Christianity as beyond redemption and that many feminists see the church as a tool of repression—certainly not a place where women are valued and where they are free. Eve, they would say, did not fall. She was pushed.

This is a long way from the breathtakingly radical manner in which Jesus treated women: dealing with the woman taken in adultery; breaking taboos when taking water from the Samaritan woman at the well or allowing himself to be touched by a women seeking healing (a woman, it is clear, bleeding in such a way as to be taboo under Jewish law); choosing women to be the first witnesses to the resurrection; allowing his ministry to be supported by the hospitality of women; or using the image of himself as a servant (understood well by women and rather less well by men). Even St Paul, often cast in the role of First Misogynist, could say: 'In Christ there is neither male or female.'

In recent years, the debate about women and the church has centred on issues such as authority, inclusive language and the ordination of women. Issues which have highlighted fears, insecurities and hurt. But the relationship between the church and women must be wider than this. Women are 51 per cent of the population (at least where female infanticide is not practised) and, for the most part, treated as if they were a minority. Which is why this book looks at women more closely than any of the other marginalized groups. The church, which has been, and which has been seen as, part of the problem, is also a powerful tool for being part of the solution.

A LITTLE HISTORY

When women's place in society is discussed, appeals to 'the natural order' are occasionally made, or statements of the type 'it's always been that way' are heard. The reality is that women's place in society has not always been one of subservience. There is strong evidence that in the earliest days of humankind many societies worked as matriarchies, and that the man-as-hunter was rather less important than woman-as-gatherer for the tribe. In these societies the idea of God as Earth Mother was easier to conceive of than God as Sky Father. The great sea-change in this concept seems to have begun around 1500BC.

The centrality of women in society carried on in some cultures for much longer than in others. The Celts for example, were so used to the idea of ruler as Queen that when they were presented to the Roman Emperor Claudius they assumed that Agrippina, his wife, was the ruler and consequently bowed down before her. Queens ruled Egypt, in Assyria, over the Natchez Indians in the USA and even the Jewish people were led by Deborah the judge. The women of Sparta owned two-thirds of the land and, of course, Boudicca (leader of the British Iceni), led her warriors into battle. She had 20,000 Romans crucified for the rape of her daughter. Not a lady to mess with.

As societies became more formalized, women became more confined. Solon of Athens, when he became ruler in 594BC, passed a law stopping women from leaving the house at night. An early example of 'a woman's place is in the home'. And even in Egypt, women became the property of men.

This move towards restriction did not stop individual women achieving (though sometimes resorting to disguise themselves as men to do so). Polymaths such as Ban Zhao in China in AD100 still thrived and female rulers such as 'the Julias' of Rome in AD300 could still be found. Some met with less pleasant fates. Hypatia, a Greek mathematician, inventor (or inventrix perhaps) of the astrolabe, distillation process and the hygroscope, was a scientific rationalist who met her death for this crime at the hands of Cyril of Alexandria in AD415. He had monks cut the flesh from her bones while she was still alive.

In the seventeenth century, during the English Revolution, there was a brief flowering of changing ideas about women—only to be replaced with a backlash and witch hunts. For women, the world was very nearly turned upside down. In the late eighteenth and nineteenth centuries (in the West) the struggle for women's rights truly began. Mary Wollstonecraft wrote her *Vindication of the Rights of Women* in 1792, John Stuart Mill *The Subjection of Women* in 1849 and twenty years later, in the USA, the first newsletter campaigning for the rights of women was launched. More radically, Elizabeth Stanton published *The Women's Bible* in 1895—a document which accused Christianity of giving a respectable veneer to oppression.

In this century we can see how women have been 'managed'. The First World War, in many ways, gave women the vote. The Second World War gave women the taste for, and experience of, work outside the home. That taste for work became inconvenient when men came back from war, and governments mounted sophisticated propaganda campaigns to have women return home. Which they duly did.

So what does this admittedly partisan history tell us? That there is no inevitable or natural place for women in society; women's place changes in time. That women's progress is not a ratchet-like process, forever locked into a forward position; it has, at times, moved backwards as well. And can still. Many books of the Bible were written to the background music of changing ideas, and changing fears, about how women and society should be organized. 'In your understanding,' said St Paul, 'be men' (as he would). Critical, at the very least.

IN THE PRESENT

Discussing the position of any marginalized group frequently devolves to a litany of 'awful things done to people'. So it must be said, before a similar litany is given here, that, since the 1960s, women, in the West at least, have enjoyed a greater degree of choice about their lives than ever before. Legislation giving equal opportunities and outlawing discrimination has been passed. The UK has seen a female Prime Minister and women's intellectual equality is no longer a matter of doubt.

But. There is always a but. Women are still poorer than men in every society, on every continent; in the Third World they are the poorest of the poor.

ECONOMICS AND WOMEN

Women do two-thirds of the world's work, produce 45 per cent of the world's food (in Africa they do 75 per cent of the agricultural work), own only 1 per cent of the world's property (in the USA this rises to 16 per cent) and earn one tenth of the world's income.

Women working outside the home hold down two jobs. In Tanzania, for example, men work, on average, for 1,800 hours in the fields in a year, and women 2,600; but after the field work, women begin cooking, cleaning and caring for children. In industrialized countries women work 46 hours a week in the home—plus any paid work.

The centrality of women's work in the Third World is being recognized and gender awareness is now a feature of many of the aid programmes initiated by the Overseas Development Administration. In matters of population too, some of the older, unsubtle, arguments for 'population control' are being replaced by moves towards women's education (particularly literacy) and primary health care—both of which make a significant impact on women's ability to control their own fertility.

Even with legislation for equal pay for equal work in the UK, women earn only 70 per cent of men's income. Many jobs for women are low-paid, part-time and do not qualify women for state benefits. Six out of ten women work full-time and more than two-thirds (67 per cent) of women with children aged five do so. Most women work because they need to, but women with children who choose not to work outside the home (only one in six households are of this type) are described in data as 'economically inactive'—which is probably one of the more calculated insults to the work of women.

Management and the professions remain dominated by men. In medicine and the professions, men outnumber women 2:1 and this rises to 4:1 for the legal profession. The latter is a particular matter of concern when judges are capable of suggesting that the perpetrator of a rape should bear the 'penalty' of buying a holiday for his victim as a 'sentence' or that an eight-year-old child who was sexually abused was not blameless. Both were recent legal judgments—by men, one hardly need add. It was only in 1991 that women owned their own

bodies in marriage; before this marital rape was legitimate and called a 'right'. The law allows no 'self-defence' defence for women who have been systematically abused and who, in response, kill their husbands.

EDUCATION

The history of education reads much like any other history for women. British universities could first accept women, if they wished, in 1875. Oxford actually did so in 1920. In 1919 the Sex Disqualification Removal Act removed barriers to women entering the civil professions but by 1948 there were no women in London Medical Schools—eventually a quota was imposed of 15 per cent. Currently, only 11 per cent of university teachers are women and less than 2 per cent hold professorships.

This has all changed now in schools, of course? Not really. Girls are still classified as to what they can and cannot do by gender. One study shows that this happens, on average, forty times a day. There are still academic prejudices. Research from the USA has shown that exactly the same paper, one given a female name and the other male, results in the perceived-male paper gaining higher grades. Similarly, teachers routinely gave male students two-thirds of their time, and male students complain if this ever falls below 40 per cent.

Two-thirds of the people in the world who cannot read are women.

HEALTH AND MEDICINE

Perhaps because of male domination of the medical profession, women have suffered badly. As our mental hospitals empty we increasingly find that women were incarcerated for having children out of marriage, for being 'loose' or because they masturbated. Perhaps they were lucky. Until 1936 doctors here were removing the female clitoris as a cure for masturbation.

It is in the field of mental health that women have perhaps faired worse. In this century two-thirds of lobotomies were performed on women.

Two-thirds of tranquillizers and anti-depressants are prescribed to women. Women are twice as likely to be diagnosed with clinical depression as men. Women outnumber men (roughly 11:8) in psychiatric hospitals. Women are more likely to be diagnosed as having a mental disorder when the cause is physical and are more likely to be treated on a psychiatric ward when they have a drugs or alcohol problem.

The more conventional interpretation for this would have women as 'weaker' than men. Organizations such as the mental health charity MIND take a different view. It is often women's lives, not women's minds, which need to be changed. Or as female patients in the US would say, the need is to 'break out—not down'. Male domination in this field also has some rather subtle effects: the cattle markets of ante-natal clinics or the insertion of IUDs without anaesthetic, for example. Medical testing is another area where women are forgotten. Testing of low-cholesterol diets in the USA, and the advice which followed for us all, were based entirely on studies of men, as were tests for the efficacy of aspirin as a preventive measure for heart disease. This despite the fact that heart disease is the biggest killer of post-menopausal women. Women's biology is often regarded as 'too complicating' in testing. Which means that half the human race is too complicated.

VIOLENCE

Women live in a violent world—at least a world where violence is done to them. In Britain it is estimated that 1 in 10 children is sexually abused (in America the estimates are higher). 8 out of 10 of these children are girls; 99 per cent of the perpetrators are men.

In Britain nearly half of all murdered women are killed by their partners. In 1991, there were 1,500 men under sentence for rape in Britain. Statistics on domestic violence are not kept by the Home Office although various surveys in the USA put the figures at anywhere between one in twenty and one in four relationships. A Scottish survey puts the incidence at 25 per cent. In other countries the rate is higher—50 per cent in Thailand, and perhaps as high as 80 per cent in Ecuador; in Papua New Guinea it was called 'an accepted custom' during parliamentary debate. In countries where women are not valued, the birth of a female child is more than a disappointment. In Europe and the USA (where male and female babies are equally valued) the ratio of female to male babies is 1.06:1. Even where women are dying of malnutrition in sub-Saharan Africa the ratio is 1.01:1. A population which has more males:females has usually done so by design; often by female infanticide. In India the female to male ratio is now 0.92:1. In 1991 a UN report noted the elimination of females in India, Pakistan, China, Albania and the United Arab Emirates (in the latter the female to male ratio was 0.48:1). In 1982 one province of China had 503 boys to every 100 girls.

WOMEN AND THEIR BODIES

When a women's life depends on becoming married, the question of what will fit 'men's taste' becomes a preoccupation. In China, for centuries, women had their feet bound over to make them small and a delight to men. The feet were so terribly distorted that women could not walk and, should the bandages be removed for any great length of time, the pain was unbearable, sometimes to the point of death.

The West was, and is, no exception. Women were supposed to be quiet and biddable—instruments as the 'scold's bridle' saw to that. The bridle has become a source of humour nowadays; its cousin 'the branks' was rather less amusing—this induced silence by dragging women around until blood ran out. Women risked their health to acquire the hour-glass shape beloved of the Edwardians and, at a time of the most basic surgery, sometimes had ribs removed.

Today, thousands of young women starve themselves with anorexia or purge themselves with bulimia to fit notions of what a woman

65

should be. At any one time in the USA, 50 per cent of the female population are dieting. In her book *The Beauty Myth* (heavy on conspiracy theory though it is) Naomi Wolf points out that the same women who have starved their flesh away later resort to breast implants to give themselves shape.

For millions of women in Africa and in Arabia the idea of conforming to an acceptable shape for marriage has much more sinister connotations. Sometimes called 'female circumcision', female genital mutilation is a reality for between 90–100 million women living today. Although principally a feature of Muslim countries, it also occurs amongst Christians—notably in Kenya.

It can take three main forms: sunna, excision and infibulation. In sunna 'circumcision', the sheath and tip are cut away from the clitoris. In excision the whole clitoris is cut away—as, usually, are the inner lips surrounding the vagina. Infibulation is the most severe form. The clitoris and sheath and the labia minora are removed and the flesh scraped from the labia majora. These are then sewn together—or pinned together by thorns—and a small stick inserted to produce a tiny hole for menstrual blood and urine to escape. The legs are bound together from hip to ankle for around forty days to allow the wound to heal.

This process usually happens to girls of between the ages of five and eight. The operation is carried out by a 'wise' woman and the girl is held down by other women during the process. There is no anaesthetic. The tools of the operation are usually glass shards, iron blades or sharpened stone. On marriage, the girl (if she lives) may need to be cut open, and the same situation applies in childbirth.

Why do women do this? Because without it their daughters are unmarriageable. In some cases there are more worrying reasons. In Kenya both Muslim and Christian women have been told that without this they will not see Paradise. In 1992 the World Health Organization took a stand against female genital mutilation. Until then, the WHO had feared the tag of cultural imperialism.

It is because of the history of the control and abuse of women's bodies by others that the control of fertility has become such a central issue to feminists, and why the continuing opposition by the Roman Catholic church to contraception is such a source of pain and anger. For many Christians, abortion is a harder issue to consider, and yet this too is seen by women as a debate about who owns a woman's body, quite as much as about the rights of the foetus.

Women's bodies are used to sell everything from soap to cars and when selling the product ends, the bodies themselves become the focus of attention in pornography. From page three and the top shelf at the newsagents to centres for hard-core porn, women are objects, not people.

WOMEN AND THE CHURCH

Despite the constraints of society, women have always had a central role in the Christian church. Meetings of the early church took place under women's roofs, and women supported the ministry of Jesus with both time and money. In the Middle Ages, the convent offered learning and release as well as vocation; powerful abbesses influenced the church and had seats in Parliament long before votes were given to women. Even when the church has been most repressive as an institution to women, it has often worked as support network at a personal level.

As we have noted before, many women feel that the church is a hopeless cause. There are four areas where this is most apparent: the priesthood/ministry, the maleness of God, 'headship' and the language of the church.

There is no space here to rehearse the arguments for and against the ordination of women—a preoccupation of Anglicans at present but perhaps just a dress rehearsal for the Roman Catholics next century—but it is worth noting that 85 Christian denominations do ordain women and 82 do not. Even those which do not ordain women have begun to take the role of women's ministry more seriously. There are now two female bishops—one Lutheran and one Episcopalian. Out of 14,000 Episcopalian priests in the USA, 1,000 are women. Non-conformist churches have a strong women's ministry. The 'maleness'—or otherwise—of God has never been a problem for Christian mystics, God being so far beyond narrow human definitions and yet so intimate in love. Biblical translators have been quicker to make exclusive assumptions. In Genesis, for example, when the phrase 'let us make man in our image' is used, the 'our' here is not the Yahweh or El male form, but the Elohim plural used for male or female. Man is also used here in its generic sense and yet what definitions of supremacy have followed from this.

Headship is also a matter of translation and interpretation. Paul uses the word *kephale* which has a wide variety of meanings in the New Testament: a cornerstone, a source or the body—or even goal or aim. To use it narrowly to mean the male-as-head is to take a very restricted view.

Language matters. It confirms stereotypes. There are a wide range of terms of abuse for women who are sexually active—none for men. Women are called after names of food: honey, tart, crumpet. How we name things reinforces our view of them. Because of this there has been a move towards inclusive language in the church.

This is one of the most contentious of issues and some of the alternatives seem to replace one set of inadequate male words, for an equally inadequate set of female words. But there certainly are areas where removing exclusive language would be quite as useful as installing inclusive language. In the Church of England the creed has the phrase 'who for us men and for our salvation came down from heaven'. The Episcopal Church in the USA simply uses 'for us and for our salvation'. Non-exclusion.

GROUP WORK

Looking at one half of humanity can never be a small task. Changes in the lives of women have sometimes taken hundreds of years to achieve—a sense of humility is required when we look at what we can do. Darcus Howe, the black rights activist, was once asked what white liberals could do for the cause of black people. 'Don't get in the way,' he said. Not-getting-in-the-way is an art which requires an open mind and self-awareness. The ideas in this section are just starting points.

A SUGGESTED FORMAT

You may find it useful for all the group to read the previous section on women. It is a long section, but half of humanity does require a little in-depth consideration.

'Looking at women' suggests ways in which your group can begin the process of setting priorities and thinking about action. The section 'The Bible and Women' gives some ideas for Bible study. 'Thinking about women' is a brief section with prayers, quotes and additional statistics to think about.

LOOKING AT WOMEN

One of the first definitions of feminism was encapsulated in the phrase 'the personal is political'. Which simply means that we all relate to each other in ways that not only have to do with who we are as individuals (as souls) but have to do with what we expect 'typical' men and women to be.

The Gospels tell us that the hairs on our head are numbered. Which is a lyrical way of saying that each one of us is cherished for our individuality by God, and is a challenge for us to do the same. Psychologists use the word 'labelling' in a very specific way—certain descriptions of people have such a strong labelling effect that it renders people incapable of seeing beyond them. The label may be 'disabled' or 'homosexual' or 'black', or it may be 'woman'. The Gospels' call for love of the individual is a long way from our tendency to label. Some of the ideas here attempt to move beyond the label.

ACTIONS

Qualities

Each member of the group lists six qualities, on a piece of paper, which they consider masculine or feminine. These should be collated together (perhaps on a flip-chart) is there any consensus? Where did we find these notions of 'typical' from? If the headings are reversed (masculine for feminine) on the chart, can we think of men and women who have these untypical qualities? What do we think of them? This is a warming-up discussion which may tell you a few things about each other.

Obligations

Men and women feel bound by their roles and this applies to church too. Churches 'oblige' men and women in different ways. Women may feel that they need to dress up or help out with the coffee, or men that they have to move the tables or be unemotional. Each person should write down one thing that they feel obliged to be at church—it doesn't have to be an irksome burden. Each 'obligation' should be put into a female or male pile and then the women take a 'male' obligation—and vice versa.

This is now a contract. Next Sunday you are now obliged to be or do what your slip of paper tells you to do. Not enough slips of paper from the men? It should tell you something.

Concerns

In small groups draw three concentric circles. In the centre write down those things which you see as the greatest concern affecting women in your church and local community. Do the same in the next circle for the country as a whole and, finally, in the outer circle for international issues. Use these priorities to discuss the areas which your group would like to take action on. Remember there is another invisible circle and that is drawn around ourselves and families—how we behave towards men and women there.

THE BIBLE AND WOMEN

When we read the Bible with an eye to women, the contrasts between the Old and New Testaments are stunning. Perhaps this is one way of beginning to understand the process of re-creation in Christ. The Old Testament certainly records strong women but the New Testament begins a process of inclusion which has not finished yet.

Exodus 19:3–5; Matthew 23:37–39. Both Moses and Jesus use mothering and nurturing ideas of God.

Judges 4 and 5. This time the image of a women as a powerful leader.

1 Samuel 22—2 Samuel 10 and Luke 1:46–56. How do these women express their joy? What do they say it means for others who follow? What does it say about God's justice?

Proverbs 31:10–31. This is the well-known passage concerning a 'capable wife' who 'rises while it is yet dark'. It is often criticized for celebrating women-as-workhorse but it is more subtle and beautiful than that: 'she is clothed in dignity and power'. What sort of wisdom writing could be constructed for the 'virtuous husband' today?

Leviticus 20:10 and John 8:1–11. Contrasting the law and the love.

John 4:7–42. The Samaritan woman at the well. By accepting water from her Jesus made himself ritually unclean. How did she react to his non-judgmental response? How should we?

Matthew 9:18–23; Mark 5:25–34; Luke 8:40–49. Amongst Jews the blood taboo was very strong and perhaps explains the woman's reluctance to be known. Once again, the 'rules' are changed for the sake of compassion.

John 11:17–27; John 20:11–18; Luke 24:1–12. The truth revealed to women who believed. **Romans 16.** This chapter gives a good idea of women's ministry in Rome. From 29 greetings, 16 are to women; Phoebe is a deacon and Priscilla a fellow worker.

Acts 9:36–42; Acts 16:14–15; Acts 18:24–26. Priscilla's work is equated with that of her husband; Dorcas and Lydia's roles are described.

1 Corinthians 14:26–36. The famous quote on women remaining silent in church. It is likely that this referred to speaking and prophesy during preaching—especially when put into the context of the rest of women's ministry in Acts and the Epistles. Even if such a liberal interpretation is taken, then this has to be set against such injunctions as **Acts 13:20–29**—which are not strictly adhered to!

THINKING ABOUT WOMEN

Review these quotations. Each person selects one or two that grab your attention (for positive or negative reasons) and discuss as a group.

By God, if women had written stories
As clerks have written their oratories
They would have written of men more
wickedness,
Than all the race of Adam may address.

Chaucer, The Wife of Bath

I thought I saw two people, but it was only a man and his wife.

Russian proverb

According to the WHO 1992 report, a baby girl born in the richest countries (1 in 8) expects to live to 81, have two children and have $1,000 a year spent on her health. A baby girl in the poorest countries (1 in 7) expects to live to 43 (1 in 3 will die before five), will have ten children and have less than $1 a year spent on her health.

Lech Walesa is the name associated with the Polish Solidarity movement. It was actually started by two women, Anna Walentynowicz and Alina Pientkowska.

This one they call a farmer; send in teachers to teach him to farm (while I'm out growing the food); lend him money (while I'm out growing the food); promise him fortunes if he'd raise cotton (while I'm out growing food). No, I daren't stop working, and I won't abandon that thing I was born for—to make sure my children have food in their bellies.

African woman farmer, 1984

If God is male, not female, then men are intrinsically better than women. It follows then, that until the emphasis on maleness in the image of God is redressed the women of the world cannot be entirely liberated. For if God is thought of as simply and exclusively male, then the very cosmos seems sexist.

Bishop Paul Moore

God created the human person—man and woman both—as part of a unified divine plan and in his own image. Men and women are therefore equals before God: equal as persons, equal as children of God, equal in dignity and equal in rights.

Pope Paul VI

In many people's imagination [the Trinity] comes down to an old man, a young man and a bird. First God is not three people, much less three males. God is better described as divine origin, source, ground of our being ... divine communicator, redeemer. . . energy, mover, transforming power.

Sister Sandra Schneiders

The harsh words he spoke were never for women ... It was the religious leaders whom he called whitewashed tombs and accused of hypocrisy; it was the greedy businessmen whom he called thieves ... Small wonder that the women loved him so much. Small wonder that after one of his disciples had betrayed him and another denied him the women were prepared to risk everything for his sake. The women were at the foot of the cross. The women were there to anoint his body on the third day. And the women were there to see the stone rolled away, the empty tomb, and the reality of the resurrection.

Elaine Storkey, What's Right with Feminism

In 1990 there was a higher percentage of women in the Indian parliament than in the US (7.9 per cent to 6.4 per cent). Women are 12.7 per cent of the world's parliaments.

The occasion was Martin Luther King's birthday. We were talking about Dr King with the children and asking them what they had discussed in school about him. Tommy said immediately, 'We were talking about how he was working for freedom for all men.' Our immediate response was, 'You mean freedom for all men and women.' 'No,' Tommy said, 'the book said men and it meant just men.'

Kathleen and James McGinnis,
Parenting for Peace and Justice

*O God for whom we long
as a woman in labour
longs for her delivery;
Give us courage to wait,
strength to push,
the discernment to know the right time;
that we may bring into the world
your joyful peace,
through Jesus Christ, Amen.*

Janet Morley

*It is the way of God
to set good against evil.
So Jesus Christ who
sets good against evil
is our real Mother.
We owe our being to him—and this is
    the essence
of motherhood!—
and all the delightful,
loving protection
which ever follows.
God is as really our Mother
as he is our Father.*

*The human mother
may put her child tenderly to
    her breast,
but our tender Mother Jesus
simply leads us
into his blessed breast
through his open side,
and there gives us
a glimpse of the Godhead
and heavenly joy
—the inner certainty
of eternal bliss.*

Julian of Norwich,
Revelations of Divine Love (1373)

ACTION ON WOMEN'S ISSUES

Attitudes to women are learned very early—but can be unlearned very late; therefore a great deal of what we can do begins with ourselves, in our homes and with our children.

ACTION IN THE HOME: THE FAMILY AND INDIVIDUALS

Breaking down stereotypes

We may not talk about sexual stereotypes very much but our actions say a great deal—especially to children. In their book *Parenting for Peace and Justice*, Kathleen and James McGinnis came up with three guidelines for parents:

◆ Help children see that their potential is not limited by their gender, especially in careers, interests and the kind of person they become. Girls are allowed to be strong, boys sensitive. Compassion and caring are qualities of both sexes.

◆ Help them understand some of the cultural forces which exist 'out there' and which oppress women and men.

◆ Help them understand what sexism is, how it works in society and how it can be changed.

Easier said than done. So what actions can be taken to make these ideas a reality? Who does what around the home? Who stays at home if the children are sick? Who arranges childcare? Who deals with teachers? Shops? Makes the food, does the laundry or ironing? Who decides how money is spent? Is responsible for discipline? Who volunteers for support activities—the PTA, Scouts, Brownies etc?

Try doing an audit on your activities. Who does what most of the time. Why?

All relationships are different, so the division of labour may vary, and one parent may stay home and have greater responsibility for running the home. Fine, but it should be made clear that this is an active choice and that when possible this changes—depending who has the time free. If you do think you share activities fairly, ask who takes responsibility for the work; if a man washes up is he helping his wife—or helping his life?

Skills

The Rastafarian poet Benjamin Zephaniah has a poem called 'Macho Man', which ends with the lines: 'Macho man. He can't cook. He can't clean. He can't sew. Macho man he in complete control.' Everyone needs some basic skills. Boys should be able to cook, clean and sew and girls really should learn how to change a plug, deal with computers, and so on.

As with adults, audit which jobs around the house boys and girls do. How often are they asked to help? Is the expectation different for girls? Why?

Minding the language

As we saw earlier, language both reflects and forms ideas. The National Union of Journalists are well aware of this and have issued guidelines about non-sexist language. This includes: firefighter rather than fireman; manning—staffing; chairman—chairperson; spokesman—official/representative; manmade—synthetic; man in the street—citizen, etc. Do we tell girls they are pretty and little boys they are strong/clever?

Toys for the boys

Meccano and trains, skateboards and Nintendo. Nowadays a girl can have it all ... See also the section in the chapter 'War, Violence and Peace' about 'Violent toys'.

Permission

We all give strong signals about what we find acceptable and unacceptable. Friends quickly know what is 'permitted' in our house. This does not mean oppressive political correctness or a humourless home but it can mean knowing that sexism is unacceptable to us.

Images

On average we watch television for twenty-three hours a week; national newspapers sell sixteen million copies every day. During Live Aid, when a film showing a starving child was shown (running against a soundtrack of the Car's song, 'Drive') the switchboard jammed. When Michelle in *EastEnders* decided against an abortion, doctors reported other women doing the same. The media influence us. As we have seen, the NUJ are aware of bias in news (which does not stop it happening) but it is much harder to deal with in fictional programmes. These are some questions to ask:

◆ are women seen as in control or as victims?

◆ are they 'rescued' by men?

◆ all size ten? (in real life 47 per cent of women are size sixteen and over)

◆ are they white or able-bodied?

◆ are they all young?

In particular, comedy and advertising trade on stereotypes. The images can be obvious: the Supermodels advert for cars or Ariel soap powder are cases in point. In the latter, the advert featuring housewives had women who did not know that 'butter was fat' whilst a male clothes designer went off to have his powder 'scientifically tested'. Try monitoring adverts in magazines and papers for a week. Do the same with a favourite comedy show. What are they saying about women? If you don't like it— complain (see 'Resources'). Do camera angles make male products look 'strong' or is soft focus used for female products?

ACTION IN THE COMMUNITY: NEIGHBOURHOOD AND CHURCH

The church

Depending on your denomination, awareness will be found at different levels. As with bullying in schools, if someone says, 'we don't have a problem here', they probably do. The following is a list of possible actions in the church.

Questions

◆ Who runs the church? How many women are there on church committees?

◆ Are all committees the same or are some more male/female than others? Why?

◆ Are there men on the coffee rota, the cleaning and flower rota? Why not?

◆ Who reads the lessons?

◆ Who leads the intercessions?

◆ Have you looked at non-exclusive language?

Activities

◆ Support the Women's World Day of Prayer

◆ Focus on the work of women in the church on Stewardship Sunday

◆ Celebrate Juliantide (8 May)

◆ Think about supporting organizations such as Forward and Women's Aid (see 'Resources')

◆ Try as a group monitoring the media for a week.

School and workplace

Questions to ask:

◆ Does the school or workplace have an equal opportunities policy?

◆ Is training given to staff in gender (and race) awareness?

◆ How many female managers are there? What proportion is this of the workforce?

◆ How many women are there on the School Board of Governors and the PTA? Half?

◆ Are teachers aware of the research on gender and attention time given by teachers?

◆ Are exam papers marked without reference to name (that is, number coded)?

◆ Are teachers taught to deal with stereotyping in resource materials?

◆ Do teachers ever ask questions such as 'Can I have two strong boys to carry this'?

◆ Is media studies on the school curriculum?

ACTION FOR THE NATION AND WORLD

Once again, at this level a great deal of what is possible is through lobbying, writing to MPs and the media. Because 'women's issues' cross so many fields: education, pension rights, media representation, poverty and gender and benefits rights (to name a few), the most realistic response is to tackle these issues, one by one, through the range of organizations listed here (and elsewhere in this book) and through MPs and MEPs.

But change begins with individuals. They say that the hand that rocks the cradle rules the world. Not yet, but not for want of trying.

RESOURCES

Voluntary organizations will supply a publications list if SAE is provided.

The Fawcett Society 40–46 Harleyford Rd, London, SE11 5AY. A membership organization campaigning for equal rights for women. Has particular expertise on gender causes of poverty, unequal employment rights, pension rights, tax law and childcare provision.

Change PO Box 824, London, SE24 9JS. Has an international focus on women's rights.

Women's Aid Federation PO Box 391, Bristol, BS99 7WS. The national umbrella organization of women's refuges. There are 200 voluntarily funded refuges in the UK. Supplies a basic fact sheet on women and violence.

The National Alliance of Women's Organisations 279–281 Whitechapel Rd, London, E1 1DY. An umbrella organization for women's groups; publishes a range of briefings on rural women, women and the EC, women and development and others.

Forward 38 King's St, London, WC2E 8JT. Works to inform people about female genital mutilation and to support and advise women.

The ITC handles complaints about ITV, Channel 4, cable and satellite television. 70 Brompton Rd, London, SW3 1EY.

The Radio Authority handles complaints about commercial (independent) radio. Holbrook House, 14 Great Queen St, London, WC2B 5DG.

Broadcasting Standards Council considers complaints about privacy, decency, violence and sexual conduct on radio, TV and advertisements. 5–8 The Sanctuary, London, SW1P 3JS.

Mother's Union Media Awareness Project 24 Tufton St, London, SW1P 3RB.

The Press Complaints Commission deals with all press complaints. 1 Salisbury Square, London, EC4Y 8AE.

The Advertising Standards Authority handles complaints about advertising in magazines and newspapers. Brook House, Torrington Place, London, WC1E 7HN.

Publications For the Banished Children of Eve by SCM Press (£1.50). A series of articles looking at theology from a female, and very approachable (not jargon-filled) point of view. Essential reading. Also gives a more extensive reading list on women and Christianity.

What's Right With Feminism?, Elaine Storkey, SPCK. The place of women looked at from a Christian, feminist, perspective. A balanced book which makes an excellent introduction to the subject.

The War Against Women, Marilyn French, Penguin. This does not pretend to be a 'balanced' book but is probably the most comprehensive—and readable—look at the world, as if women mattered.

A Women's History of the World, Rosalind Miles, Paladin. The worm's eye view of history (or her story).

Parenting for Peace and Justice, Kathleen and James McGinnis, Orbis. A practical guide by a family who have for ten years worked towards a peaceful and just way of Christian living.

Possessing the Secret of Joy, a novel by Alice Walker, Jonathan Cape. A terrible and wonderful book which looks at female genital mutilation.

5 WAR, VIOLENCE AND PEACE

▮ AS WE ARE

Watching the evening news or reading the morning paper can leave us feeling utterly powerless in the face of the stories of war, violence and abuse of power that assail us. When we are presented with pictures from Northern Ireland or Bosnia the urge to switch off mentally is very great. And this violence is not confined to 'somewhere else'; violence comes much closer to home, in crimes of assault, murder and rape, in child abuse, and in bullying and intimidation.

In the decade 1981 to 1991, crimes of violence doubled—as did burglary and vandalism; rape, measured over the same period, quadrupled (Social Trends 1992). Those who belong to marginalized groups are more at risk from some crimes than others. People of Afro-Caribbean origin are more likely to be the victims of burglary than the white population, and Asian families have twice the risk of vandalism, also compared with the white population. In the words of the Office of Population Census and Surveys: 'for many types of crime, ethnic minority groups are more at risk than the white population. [After social factors have been accounted for] ... the risk of being a victim of crime tends to be higher among the ethnic groups.' Many in these groups see these crimes as being racially motivated. It comes as no surprise that women are predominantly the victims of violent crimes rather than the perpetrators; 42 per cent of all women who were murdered were killed by their partners. In 1991, there were 1,500 men under sentence for rape.

The murder in 1993 of a young child, Jamie Bulger (by two other children under twelve years of age), caused every newspaper and every discussion programme on radio and television to ask how, and why, such a thing could happen. Perhaps for the first time in years people began asking themselves about moral values, about images of violence, about deprivation and family life, and about the capacity each of us has within us for violence.

As Christians we have to perform a delicate balancing act between compassion and common sense. On the one hand we have Christ's injunctions 'love your enemies, and pray for your persecutors' and 'if someone slaps your right cheek, turn and offer him your left'; and on the other we have the need to find practical ways of working out that love in society, without endangering the innocent.

▮ CHRISTIANS, WAR AND PEACE

Throughout the centuries Christians have responded in different ways to violence—most clearly in terms of war. In the early church, what we would now call pacifism was the norm. In the period AD100–300, writings of the early Church Fathers articulated in words what had long been the case in practice. Lactantius for example, wrote:

When God prohibits killing, He not only forbids us to commit brigandage, which is not allowed even by public laws; but he warns us that not even those things which are regarded as legal among men are to be done. And so it will not be lawful for a just man to be a soldier . . .

By the time of the Emperor Constantine, Christianity had made its way into the higher echelons of the Roman Empire and, by AD323, Constantine had himself become a Christian and gained control over the whole empire, and the cross had appeared on war shields and banners. In AD314, the Synod of Arles stated that Christians were now free to become soldiers.

The debate has carried on within the church. So much so that groups such as the Amish, the Mennonites, the Quakers and others have made non-violence central to their Christian faith. In 1660 the American Society of Friends declared:

We utterly deny all outward wars and strife, and fightings with outward weapons, for any end, or under any pretence whatsoever; this is our testimony to the whole world . . . The spirit of Christ, by which we are guided, is not changeable, so as once to command us from a thing as evil . . . will never move us to fight and war against any man with outward weapons, neither for the Kingdom of Christ nor for the kingdoms of this world . . . Therefore, we cannot learn war any more.

This was before the Holocaust. Many people who had come through the butchery of the First World War (60,000 men died in a day at the Somme) resolving never to engage in another war, came to the Second World War in a different frame of mind. And the question which haunts many students of that period is 'had Hitler been opposed earlier (when he took over the Rhineland) would 6 million Jews and millions of gypsies, trades unionists and others be alive today?' Is this a case when taking up arms early would have been the most loving thing to do? Many Christians take the view that 'all evil has to do to triumph is for good people to do nothing' and thus pacifism is not always a practical option. Those who are pacifists say that society is geared to war-bound thinking and that only by changing the values in society and methods of conflict resolution—'not learning war anymore'—can wars ever be avoided.

This question of militarism isn't merely an academic question for Christians in peace time. As a society we have to decide whether to consent to our taxes being spent on weapons, or violence being done in our name, and whether we take the whole business of non-violent conflict resolution seriously. Do we fund peace as lavishly as we fund war? Since 1979, Great Britain has engaged in two main military actions, the Falklands War and the conflict in the Gulf—all with varying degrees of public (and religious) support. The question which we need to ask ourselves is, 'What kind of judgments, what kind of processes should we as Christians use to make decisions about giving our consent?'

In the fourth century AD Saint Augustine turned his mind to this very problem and began to work out what is known as the criteria for a just war—all of which must be satisfied for the term 'just' to apply:

◆ it must be just in intent (in order to establish a just settlement)

◆ it must be just in disposition (that is, with no hatred for the enemy)

◆ it must be just in its auspices (waged only by those in lawful authority)

◆ it must be just in conduct (there must be no wanton violence, action must only be sufficient to achieve an end, and non-combatants must not suffer)

◆ it must not inflict great damage on the world at large.

By these criteria, if by no others, many Christians have taken the view that nuclear weapons could never, ever, be a part of a 'just war' and that some of the recent conflicts we have engaged in are not, by this definition, just. Others, such as the Quakers, would be offended at the very notion of such a concept as a 'just war' at all.

War is always costly—not only in the human lives lost in conflict, but in opportunity costs to the nation. What else could we have done with the money which we decided to spend on war—or defence? Trident, for example, with the explosive power of 4,000 Hiroshima bombs, will cost £1.4 million a day for twenty years. Every year the world spends $1,000,000,000,000—a trillion dollars—on arms; UNICEF calculates that the amount of money needed to meet the basic human needs of everyone on earth is $500,000,000 (half that sum) over the next ten years.

Spending on weapons has not reduced the number of wars—there were 127 in the period 1945–89 and the numbers are increasing.

▌ RESPONDING TO VIOLENCE

There are some occasions when violence in society is a response to violence done to that community—not so much sinning, as sinned against. The triumph of Gandhi in India was a triumph of non-violence—as was that of Martin Luther King in the USA, and they stand as testaments to the power of non-violent direct action, but others (such as Malcom X in the USA and the ANC in South Africa) have decided that the only response to institutionalized violence and oppression is self-defence; violence if necessary.

Dom Heldar Camara (retired Archbishop of Recife, Brazil) has described something which he called the spiral of violence. It begins with the imposition of institutional violence (poverty, racism, economic exploitation), followed by retaliation in the form of counter-violence (violent resistance, sabotage, terrorism, the struggle for more just conditions) and in turn the state responds with further repression (loss of civil liberties, torture, dictatorship) which feeds, once again, into the system that maintains institutional violence. And so the spiral winds round another turn.

Breaking any vicious circle is difficult, not just on the national scale, but at the personal level too. Workers now estimate that 1 in 10 children suffer from abuse (sexual and physical) and that as many as 1 in 10 old people who are dependent on a carer in the family are abused. Abuse may very well be learned in the family—in fact there is hardly a better place to learn it—and children who have themselves been victims of abuse are more likely to be abusers themselves. Which is not to say that we are doomed to perpetuate the violence inflicted on us; one of the joys of Christianity is the hope of that liberation and freedom which allows us to be what we can be, rather than what we were. As we move closer to the family, violence becomes more difficult to discuss. In their book *Parenting for Peace and Justice*, Kathleen and James McGinnis make the analogy between the spiral of violence in society and violence in the home. Not an abusive home, but in an ordinary home:

And many children have first-hand experience of living in a dictatorship. They often know what it means experientially to have someone else control your life, to be given no room to grow or to make decisions. They can begin to understand why someone or some group might strike out, even if the method seems counterproductive. This is a beginning in understanding the effects of institutional violence.

If children learn that violence works, that violence controls, then violence will be seen as a successful strategy. The message is that violence is OK. And this is where the whole thorny question of corporal punishment must be raised. Certainly, the Old Testament has several references on the theme of 'sparing the rod and spoiling the child' and some Christians have been strong supporters of corporal punishment. But should not the compassion of Jesus for children be understood first?

Some would say at this point that surely it is better to punish a child rather than let that child become an individual who is out of control. Kathleen and James McGinnis point out that, although they had spanked their children, they came to agree with conclusions of the Gilmartin Report that children who are regularly spanked are less articulate and more sullen, have greater social distance between family members; that spanking is associated with low self-esteem; that violence begets violence; and that these children develop an overdependence on external controls. In short, it is counterproductive. The authors go on to say that not using physical punishment does not mean giving up discipline (which children need, and is part of feeling secure) but that other methods of discipline—and taking the time to create situations where the situation need not arise—is a more positive step forward. In the section 'Action on violence' some of these ideas are outlined.

Whether we are considering violence in the home, in society or between nations, the Bible makes clear that peace and justice are two sides of the same coin: 'these things you should do: Speak the truth to one another. In the courts give real justice—the kind that brings peace' (Zechariah). To avoid a just war, we first need a just peace.

▓ IMAGES

We gain our images of what is acceptable from our families, from our peers and from the media.

Anyone who has experience of children as a group will know that how the group behaves and how individuals behave are two very different things. The group's values may be much harsher and more violent than those of the individuals in the group. Individuals within the group feel bound by these values—psychologists call this 'group compliance'. The momentum of the group can be very great and its manifestations, from a riot to bullying in schools, can take many forms. We are only just beginning to understand the scale of bullying in our schools, but at its worst it can result in childhood and teenage suicide. Giving children the skills to deal with this pressure and creating

an atmosphere of trust to encourage disclosure are just two counter measures which we can take.

Violence in the media draws a great deal of criticism. A recent report (Aston University for the *News at Ten*) found that there were a hundred scenes of violence a night on TV—more than half in drama/film form (but that this was actually less than ten years ago). In the USA, an average teenager has seen 26,000 deaths on screen by the time they are sixteen. Whether there is a causal link between violence on the screen and violence on the streets is a hotly debated issue. Certainly some American psychologists think that there is, and even those who do not have begun to believe that violence on TV both reduces guilt about violence and in some way 'normalizes' it.

GROUP WORK

There are so many issues surrounding violence—from violence in ourselves, in families, in our local community, to war/pacifism and institutionalized violence, that looking for what we can do becomes a formidable task. But each of us brings our own experience of the world to the group, and these experiences can be used to discover the things which we consider to be the most important in our lives and the most appropriate for our group to work on.

In particular, your group may wish to ensure that it includes those people who are not male, white and middle class and whose experience of society (and violence in society) is harder to discover. You may also want to work with the organizers of youth activities in the church in order to hear the experiences of younger people.

It can be useful meeting with those who have experience working with these issues: Quakers, local police, organizers of women's safe houses, juvenile magistrates, NSPCC workers, Amnesty International, peace organizations and people who have taken part in non-violent direct action and who work at peaceful conflict resolution (the Peace Pledge Union or the Fellowship of the Reconciliation should be able to help with this).

A great many people are trying to make peace but that has already been done. God has not left it for us to do; all we have to do is enter into it.

D.L. Moody

A SUGGESTED FORMAT

You may find it useful for all the group to read the previous section on war, violence and peace. This is a very general section for an enormous topic, but it may trigger thoughts in the group. In a following section, 'Thinking about violence', there are additional stories, quotes, facts, poems and prayers and these can be used later as part of the discussion or now as triggers before coming together to look at the group's priorities.

The section 'The Bible and peace and justice' looks at general principles concerning violence, war and peace.

'Looking at violence' suggests ways in which your group can begin the process of setting priorities and thinking about action.

LOOKING AT VIOLENCE

The fist game

This game is a good way of breaking the ice and at the same time discovering something about conflict, co-operation and the other people in the group.

The group splits into pairs and each person in the pair faces his or her partner. At an agreed signal, each person puts both hands in front of him or her—either palms facing or in a fist. If both people make fists, each scores one point. If both partners put palms up, each scores two points. If one person puts up fists, and the other palms, then the person with the fists takes three points. After ten rounds each person should total his or her score.

The group comes back together and scores are given. Now the partnership scores are totalled. If the partnership score had been the first aim, would it have made any difference to the strategy? Pairs can try the exercise again to see.

81

Threats to peace

The group breaks into small groups and each group marks out three concentric circles out on the paper. At the centre write down what you think of as threats to peace in the neighbourhood. Working outwards, look at what you consider to be the threats to peace in the nation and, finally, do the same for the international community.

This process could take some time, especially when looking at larger issues such as international threats to peace where wider considerations of economic exploitation, defence versus aggression arise. This is where having previous input and information from others can be useful.

Come together and discuss which of the issues raised by your group you feel most motivated to work on. You may not be able to do this in one session and need to come back to it after going away and thinking around the issues.

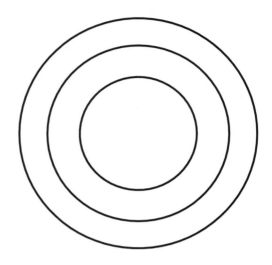

Personal experience of violence

If the group feels very at ease with itself and all the members know one another well, looking at violence in ourselves and the family can be discussed in the previous exercise, but it may be that experiences are too personal to do so. In this case it can be a good idea to get each person to write down three things: how they feel threatened; what makes them feel angry—and what might make them feel they want to lash out; and if they have experienced violence either as a child or as an adult. You may want read out some of the quotes and prayers from the 'Thinking about violence' section before starting this exercise.

One person should then collect the papers and group: the threats, the causes and the experiences. Some common experiences may emerge which can be incorporated into the group's other discussions and decision making on taking action on violence.

THE BIBLE, PEACE AND JUSTICE

1 Samuel 8:1–13. The Jewish people had decided that their future lay with a king—as other nations, rather than reliance on God's law. What are today's equivalents?

Isaiah 22:1–17. The principles of Godly rule. What does this have to say about military policy, Third World development and relief, and government policy?

Isaiah 31. The whole chapter develops the theme of reliance on God. Does reliance on God imply inaction on our part? If not, how should we act? How do we move away from military might? What is real security?

Amos 1:6–9; 5:10–15. Amos was the first biblical prophet to be recorded at length and wrote in the middle of the eighth century BC at a time of great piety and prosperity, but he could see that the prosperity was based on the exploitation of the poor. In the first chapter he sets out how the nation has exploited others. How does institutionalized sin endanger peace? How can the cycle be broken? What did God condemn through Amos and what action did he demand?

Psalm 140. Feeling overwhelmed by the prospect of violence is clearly no new phenomenon.

Isaiah 2:1–5; John 14:27–31. The great promises of peace. How do we share the vision and help peace become a reality? What does it mean for family life?

Matthew 5:1–10, 23–48. The beatitudes and the Sermon on the Mount. The most challenging calls to peace by Jesus; in personal actions and in what is demanded of a Christian society. Can we ever not turn the other cheek? Do peacemakers ever have to declare war?

Matthew 20:20–28. Authority as service.

Ephesians 4:15–16; 6:1–4. Paul explores the concept of peace in the body of Christ—from the church to the mutual respect between parents and children.

Acts 5:27–32. When must we obey God's law rather than the state's?

Romans 12:16–21. Is this how we behave to our enemies? How can we respond, how can the state respond?

James 3:13—4:3. James, as ever, practical in his advice. How does our church measure up to this? What are the characteristics of the 'wisdom from heaven' and what does James compare it with? To what extent are the causes of war similar to the causes of hostility between friends—where does the comparison end?

1 Corinthians 13:1–13; 2 Corinthians 13:11. The inspirational call to love and the expression of it.

THINKING ABOUT VIOLENCE

Review these quotations. Discuss ways in which personal violence (or pacifism) and institutional violence relate—to each other and to Christian ideals.

Close to home

There are 48,000 children on child protection registers in the UK—4 in every 1,000 children. One fifth suffered physical abuse, 1 in 10 sexual abuse and 1 in 8 neglect. There are 60,000 children in care (Social Trends 1991).

If we don't want violence to overcome the whole planet, we must begin by rooting it out at home, in our own selves. The violence in each of us is our beam; we can see nothing as long as we accept it in front of our eyes.

Jean Goss

In 1991 there were nearly 7,000 people under sentence for violent crime in the UK and a further 1,500 for rape.

How a family demonstrates affection, shares power and responsibility, resolves conflicts, responds to hostility, copes with illness and injury, expresses grief, encourages achievement, conducts its common meals, spends time and money, plans its vacation and travel, forms its political opinions, confronts fear of the future and worships—or fails to worship—God: these questions make the family the potential greenhouse of all peacemaking.

Methodists' Pastoral Letter 1986 (USA)

Your role in our eyes is unsurpassed. Children hear the Gospel message first from your lips. Parents who consciously discuss issues of justice in the home and strive to help children solve conflicts through nonviolent methods, enable their children to grow up as peacemakers.

US Catholics' Pastoral letter

As a child

'Go upstairs, Robert,' said my father. There was a sofa in the room where he hit me. He spoke to me first. 'This will hurt me more than it hurts you.' He actually said that. It did not seem real, it was like some schoolboy novel. What was most horrible was that he had got a bamboo cane to hit me with. Had he gone out and bought it? The cold-blooded calculation of that simple act is the thing that still bothers me . . .

'I am going to hit you six times.' His voice was cold. 'You are never going to do this again. Hold onto the back of the sofa and bend over.'

'No, Da. Please don't hit me. I'll be good now.' I still didn't really grasp what had been so bad . . .

The cane swished . . . My whole body was now entirely concentrated in those few inches of flesh. The third set my entire being into a contortion of agony.

. . . Then at the end, the bastard tried to hug me. How dare he salve his own pathetic conscience with that act of hypocrisy? If you're going to hurt someone, hurt them, but don't pretend it's love. That's perversion.

Bob Geldof, in the autobiography *Is That It?*

Resolving conflict . . . taking action

I would not give the impression that nonviolence will accomplish miracles overnight . . . But the nonviolent approach does something to the hearts and souls of those committed to it. It gives them new self-respect. It calls up resources of strength and courage that they did not know they had. Finally, it so stirs the conscience of the opponent that reconciliation becomes a reality.

Martin Luther King

The choice for Christians seems clear: we Christians are on the side of nonviolence, which is by no means a choice of weakness or passivity. Nonviolence means believing more passion-ately in the force of truth, justice and love than in the force of wars, murder and hatred.

Helder Camara

Nonviolence is not a cover for cowardice, but it is the supreme virtue of the brave.

Gandhi

First they came for the Jews and I did not speak out– because I was not a Jew. Then they came for the communists, and I did not speak out— because I was not a communist. Then they came for the trade unionists and I did not speak out—because I was not a trade unionist. Then they came for me—and there was no-one left to speak for me.

Pastor Niemoeller

We are war tax resisters because we have discovered some doubt as to what belongs to Caesar and what belongs to God

and we have decided to give the benefit of the doubt to God.

John K. Stoner, Mennonite Central Committee

War, peace and justice

If you want peace, work for justice.

Pope Paul VI

I sit on the neck of a man, having crushed him down, compel him to carry me ... though I assure myself and others that I am very sorry for him and wish to ease his burden by every means in my power—except by getting off his back.

Leo Tolstoy

It will be a great day when our schools get all the money they need and the airforce has to hold a bake sale to buy a bomber.

US Peace movement

In 1990, the UK spent 3.7 per cent of GNP on defence, that is, £346 per person.

An appeaser is one who feeds a crocodile— hoping that it will eat him last.

Winston Churchill

What is Trident?

Trident is a nuclear submarine
Which will be able to destroy
408 cities or areas at one time,
each with a blast five times more powerful
than the Hiroshima bomb.

Trident is 2,040 Hiroshimas.

One Trident can destroy any country on earth.
A fleet of 30 Trident submarines can end
life on earth.
How can anyone understand that?

Begin with a meditation:
To understand Trident, say the word
'Hiroshima'.
Say, and understand 'Hiroshima' again.
And again.
And again.
2,040 times.

Assuming you are able to understand
'Hiroshima' in one second, you will be
able to understand Trident in 34 minutes.

That is one Trident submarine.

To understand the destructive power of
the whole of the Trident fleet,
it would take you 17 hours, devoting one
second to each 'Hiroshima'.

Your meditation is impossible.
To understand 'Hiroshima' alone would
take a lifetime.

Jim Douglas

Prayers of peace

Lord make me an instrument of your peace;
Where there is hatred, let me sow love;
Where there is injury, pardon;
Where there is doubt, faith;
Where there is despair, hope;
Where there is darkness, light;
Where there is sadness, joy.

O Divine Master,
grant that I may not so much seek to be
understood as to understand;
to be loved as to love;
for it is in giving that we receive,
it is in pardoning that we are pardoned,
it is in dying that we are born to eternal life.

St Francis

God, creator and holy Spirit,
give me the grace to
follow the way of Jesus:

to resist evil without violence
but with my whole being;
to accept suffering
rather than inflict it;

to strive for Peace in the world
beginning in my own heart;
and to live in the Joy, simplicity
and compassion of the Gospel.

Prayer of nonviolence, Pax Christi

ACTION ON VIOLENCE

GENERAL POINTS

It is likely that during the discussions, Bible study and activities, your group will have identified an issue about which you feel strongly and on which you want to act. This section aims at helping you do just that by organizing ideas into family and home; the local community (which includes the church); national and international issues.

On the other hand, you and your group may not be at the stage of acting upon ideas yet and may need further input from some of the organizations suggested earlier (and listed in the 'Resources' section). Whatever stage your group is at, you will have already done real work in thinking about how you as individuals deal with conflict. All those who work on conflict resolution agree that declaring peace begins by declaring peace within oneself, and so the very process of discussion has been a major part of the action.

ACTION IN THE HOME: THE FAMILY AND INDIVIDUALS

Expressing anger

Everyone gets angry. It's healthy—in fact an organization campaigning for mental health in the USA has the slogan 'break out, not down'. How we choose to express anger is another matter entirely and every family does it differently. Some suppress anger and pretend it doesn't exist, others 'save up' the anger and then spend it all at once in an angry splurge, and others lash out or become depressed. Gloomy stuff? There are positive ways forward.

We can learn to express anger and to distinguish between assertiveness and aggression by making statements in the form of 'I' rather than 'you'. For example, 'You are foul when you do that' is the type of expression guaranteed to make the other person feel on the defensive—and very likely to respond in a similar way. If, on the other hand, the same feelings are expressed as 'I really feel awful when x, y or z happens' is used, there is less likelihood of a defensive response—or of escalation. Most important of all, the other person has a better chance of really hearing what you have to say. 'I' statements are also more useful with children than statements of the 'why did you . . ?' type; often the child genuinely does not know 'why', or is too embarrassed to explain childish curiosity ('I just wanted to see what happened') or simply does not have the language to explain. 'Why?' often closes rather than opens a discussion.

All this isn't to pretend that some people don't have shorter fuses than others—but rather that these 'fuses' can be encouraged to grow! The family may know (and occasionally play on) one member with a short temper. Only practice and time changes this. With both adults and children, a useful strategy is consciously to praise people when they hold their temper and manage to say what's wrong—using slightly different forms of words for adults and children. Some people might prefer to signal praise by touch, or smile. Fine. Also remember that humour (if you can manage it) is a great anger sponge—it soaks up anger in enormous quantities. Not that it should contrive to help us avoid talking about what makes us angry, but rather that it gives an opportunity for any escalation to stop.

Building a family community of non-violence

In their book *Parenting for Peace and Justice—ten years later*, Kathleen and James McGinnis reviewed what had worked, and what had not worked, with their children in their attempts to take action in the family on violence. Below are listed some of their key points. They make the point that it all does take time and effort—but works. The following are a few basic principles.

87

Affirmation. Praise is always more effective than criticism. The family may decide that there should be a special way or time do this for significant events. There should be a habit of giving praise. Plenty of physical affection is a necessary part of affirmation as is taking time to be with each child as an individual.

Co-operation. Losing rigidity, being playful, builds the atmosphere which allows non-violence to flourish. Not always an easy option, says McGinnis; 'Despite my residual rigidity we are experiencing the truth of . . . the observation that playfulness, openness and love go together. So do rigidity and violence.'

Three parent promises have been suggested to help with this:

◆ never saying 'no' when we can possibly say 'yes'

◆ when we are with our children, really being with them

◆ truly trying to see things from a child's point of view.

Co-operation can be built into a range of tasks, from gardening to recycling, and this minimizes the excessive competition which can lead to conflict. Of course we have to be realistic; children live in a very competitive world, but what we can do is give them an alternative model of how things can be made to work.

Communication. Certain forms of communication are more productive than others:

◆ using 'action terms'—the 'I statements' which were explained above

◆ being specific about what is going wrong rather than making a general criticism of another person

◆ expressing feelings honestly and saying what you want to happen

◆ listening actively—repeating back what you have heard from the other person to make sure that you have really understood them

◆ listening without judging—there is no 'right thing to say' only the thing which has to be said.

Ideas for conflict avoidance

◆ When a conflict is child-to-child, and it is verbal, then staying out of the conflict and allowing the children to resolve it themselves is often the best way forward.

◆ Changing the environment by: making use of stimulating toys to avoid boredom during the day and switching to calming activities nearer bedtime; simplifying things—making it easier for children to do things without risking some precious possession; distracting them away from unhelpful activity and planning ahead.

◆ Having expectations of children which are reasonable and using other parents, teachers, etc. to act as a 'sanity check' to see if they are reasonable.

◆ Taking time to organize the enjoyable things with children which act as a balance to the inevitable difficulties, and finding time to do things which parents want to do.

◆ Considering having regular family meetings.

Discipline. Always difficult, always necessary.

◆ Avoid punishment where possible; this isn't the soft option. It means making sure the child understands that something has gone wrong and that apologies need to be made.

◆ Try to get the children to find ways out of their behaviour—a note to themselves about chores, or homework etc.

◆ If punishment is necessary it should be as close in time as possible and appropriate; for example, if someone is consistently late in, they miss the meal, family treats etc.

◆ The rule should be that discipline is for the children, not for us. It must be about helping them, not getting rid of our anger. Avoid spanking.

Violent toys

Many toys, especially for boys, glorify violence—everything from guns and Action Man to macho cartoon hero games and warships and jet fighters. Not only do they begin to reinforce the idea that 'violence is OK' but they also reinforce some of the male stereotypes which go with that notion.

Parents have the option of choosing toys and encouraging others to buy toys which do not glorify violence. But, as with everything else, we have to live in the real world—a child is not going to become a homicidal maniac overnight because Aunty B buys him or her a gun. Also the child has to live in the world where most parents do not restrict toys in this way. This means two things. First, parents have to be wary of setting up war toys as objects of desire because of their very scarcity; and, second, a child will need to feel pretty confident about explaining the situation to friends.

This has a follow-on in the skills children will need to be taught to deal with the world; self-defence and 'street skills' are options here.

Images

Television and comics (sometimes reinforcing each other) carry images of violence; violence as much from the 'good guys' as from the 'bad guys'. The first step in countering images of violence is to watch what the children watch—and maybe discuss it with them. At which point there are further options of restricting television and also complaining to broadcasting authorities (addresses in the 'Resources' section). The Peace Pledge Union have a special 'Children and War' project which works in this area.

Avoiding 'us' and 'them'

We all can enter into an us and them mentality. One way of countering this is by pointing out how interconnected our lives are—perhaps through the countries of origin of the food we eat. What do the people do there? How do they make their living? Do the children go to school?

Become informed—you may like to read publications such as *New Internationalist* or Pax Christi's *Justpeace*.

ACTION IN THE COMMUNITY

The skills and insights which have been gained in our own lives can be transferred to other areas of life. Meetings at work might well be transformed by some of the techniques in the 'Communication' section (above) and church meetings might never be the same again . . .

Your group may have decided to look at some local community issues: racial violence, domestic violence or local crime, in which case the first step is to find out more information from people such as the social services, NSPCC offices, police or local women's refuge. Good intentions, if not carried through advisedly, can lead to making things worse than better, so be advised and work with those who know the local situation.

Your group may decide that it wants to affiliate to, or raise funds for, an organization concerned with peace and justice issues or those concerned with violence—the 'Resources' section has a list with descriptions of their work.

At church you may want to use the parish magazine or notice board to draw attention to issues which relate to peace, justice and violence. It may be as simple as passing on basic information about the costs of war or local community concerns about violence. You may also want to review how your church or diocese invests its money—are the investments ethical?

Peace Sunday is usually the last Sunday in January and the Week of Prayer for World Peace in the last week of October—your church could use this as an occasion to pray for peace. Pax Christi and the Fellowship of the Reconciliation have ideas for prayers, hymns and services.

The idea of peaceful conflict resolution and peace issues can be extended to schools. How is the idea of war portrayed at school? Are the human costs incorporated into the teaching of history?

Your children may have already experienced violence, or the threat of violence, at school in the form of bullying. All schools have difficulties with bullying—denying there is a problem is the first step in having a problem. Does your child's school have a policy on bullying? More important, how does it educate pupils about the issue?

You may decide that you want to take part in direct action—perhaps you live near a military installation to which you object or perhaps you want to lobby local shops at Christmas about war toys? Both of these need careful handling and advice—see the 'Resources' section for organizations.

ACTION FOR THE NATION AND WORLD

At this level, we are looking at government policy and how it affects our lives. Therefore action can be of the lobbying kind, writing letters to MPs and MEPs on issues which concern us and joining organizations which work at this level. There are also practical actions which some groups have decided to take.

◆ The peace tax campaign. As warfare has become more technological, there has been a move away from military conscription to economic conscription (around 12 per cent of public spending). The peace tax campaign is a response to this. People not on PAYE may choose to withhold tax (this is illegal) and others decide to covenant the equivalent to peace charities.

◆ Each year thousands of people remember the bombing of Hiroshima and Nagasaki on 6 and 9 August, drawing the public's attention to the reality of nuclear war.

◆ Writing a letter of protest with the tax return.

◆ Remembrance Sunday and the white poppy. This is sometimes seen as controversial, in that it represents an alternative to the traditional red poppy. Those organizing the white poppy remembrance are clear that it is not intended as an affront to those of our community who died in war, but rather remembers all victims of war and marks the real costs in human life without any hint of triumphalism.

▉ RESOURCES

ORGANIZATIONS

Christian organizations concerned with peace and justice issues

Fellowship of the Reconciliation (FOR) 40–46 Harleyford Rd, Vauxhall, London, SE11 5AY. A national and international ecumenical organization committed to pacifism and the advance of practical methods of non-violent conflict resolution. Publishes briefing papers and a bi-monthly newsletter, *Peacelinks*, and has local groups around the country, runs conferences and training in non-violence techniques.

Pax Christi Christian Peace Education Centre, 9 Henry Rd, London, N4 2LH. This is the international peace movement (represented in eighteen countries) based in the Roman Catholic tradition but which welcomes members from all Christians denominations and none. Has specialist advice on peace and education, each year organizes a four-day vigil for peace and publishes advice on services and prayers on the theme of peace.

Quaker Peace and Service Friends House, Euston Rd, London, NW1 2BJ. The social action arm of the Religious Society of Friends (Quakers). Publishes a range of briefings on peace issues.

Peace organizations

The Peace Pledge Union 6 Endsleigh St, London, WC1H 0DX. An organization which was formed in response to World War I, whose members sign a pledge that: 'I renounce war and I will never support or sanction another.' Runs the 'Children and War' project which focuses on war toys and messages to children about violence. Works in the UK and Europe. The PPU also organizes the white poppy remembrance each year and has an education division. Publishes the 'Children and War' newsletter.

Peace Tax Campaign 1a Hollybush Place, London, E2 9QX. The PTC aims to persuade Parliament to introduce legislation allowing people conscientiously opposed to war to have the military part of their taxes allocated to peace-building. Publishes a monthly newsletter 'Conscience' and produces a leaflet for Christians ('Are you praying for peace but still paying for war?').

Organizations involved with international justice and peace

The Campaign Against the Arms Trade 11 Goodwin St, London N4 3HQ. Researches into the arms trade and campaigns against the UK's trade in arms. Produces a monthly newsletter and special briefings.

Amnesty International 99–119 Roseberry Ave., London, EC1R 4RE. Campaigns for prisoners of conscience worldwide and against torture and the death penalty. It has 1.1 million members worldwide and has acted on behalf of more than 42,000 men and women. Network of 320 UK groups adopt prisoners of conscience, and organize an urgent action network. Publishes a number of briefings on specialist subjects including 'Religions and the Death Penalty' (£2), 'Arguments for Human Rights from the World's Religions' (£2) and 'In Prison and You Came to Me' (suggestions for sermons, services, prayers and readings, £1).

Organizations concerned with children and violence

The National Society for the Prevention of Cruelty to Children (NSPCC) 67 Saffron Hill, London, EC1N 8RS.

EPOCH 77 Holloway Rd, London, N7 8JZ. For information about alternatives, and reasons against, corporal punishment.

Television and violence

The Advertising Standards Authority Brook House, 2–16 Torrington Place, London, WC1E 7HN. Write to them if you are concerned about advertisements.

The Independent Television Commission 70 Brompton Rd, London, SW3 1EY. For complaints about violence on independent television.

The Broadcasting Standards Council For complaints about violence on TV and in advertisements.

PRINTED MATERIALS

(Please also see under 'Organizations' above)

Parenting for Peace and Justice—ten years later by Kathleen and James McGinnis. A really practical guide by parents who have worked at the issues for many years. Orbis Publishing.

Peace People by Pax Christi; probably the best organized pack for groups to work with who are interested in non-violence/civil disobedience, human rights, conscientious objection and witness. The pack uses eight people who have campaigned—and sometimes given their lives for—peace and justice. The pack has their stories, suggested discussions, Bible studies and posters. £3.50. Pax Christi also publish an extensive range of materials on fasting, prayer and almsgiving for peace; ideas for action; facts on the arms trade; co-operative games; contemplative works and works of experience. Resource list available.

Love Begins Where Violence Ends from Fellowship of Reconciliation. This is a collection of briefings—including 'Spirituality and nonviolence', 'The United Nations and Peacekeeping' and 'Pacifism in the Early Church'. Other inclusions are 'A guide to nonviolent direct action' and 'A call to nonviolence'.

The Peace Education Project: the Peace Pledge Union publishes and distributes an extensive range of materials for use in schools by primary and secondary teachers. Also PPU publishes a wide range of books on general peace issues. Send for a resources list.

Bullying, the Child's View A report based on the calls to Childline's Bullying Line. Shows how to counter bullying in schools. From Turnaround Distribution Ltd, 27 Horsell Rd, London, N5 1XL (£6 inc. p. and p).

MARGINALIZED GROUPS

It is a central tenet of Christianity that the human race is one; all are made in the image of God. In Christ, we are told, there is neither Jew nor Greek, slave nor free, male nor female.

Yet equally clearly society is riven with divisions. In particular, certain groups are excluded from the mainstream, denied access to resources, freedom or justice. Treatment of the 'outcast' is one of the crucial measures of the degree to which a society is 'wholesome'.

And yet it is also an issue for the churches directly in that they, too, often follow the model of society rather than that of the body of Christ.

It is a fact of this marginalization that those on the 'inside' are rarely aware of it, or their involvement in it. Therefore an important part of this section is for us to listen to the experience of those who are marginalized and to reflect on what they have to say.

RACISM

Racism is one of the most obvious issues in this area facing society and the church. It has been defined as 'an action or institutional structure which subordinates a person or group because of their ethnic background'. This discrimination is based on prejudice or hatred, which are in turn founded on some false generalizations about the group concerned—Afro-Caribbeans are lazy or those of Chinese origin are sly. Some stereotypes, however, hold a grain of truth, but tend to deny variations and are highly selective. They may reflect a general trend that no longer holds. They damage self-image, promote misinformation and are used to justify racist policies.

Stereotypes also trivialize important things—customs, beliefs, differences, people— 'Books don't say "I is for Italian", they say "I is for Igloos, Insects, Inkwells and Indians." Like Indians are things instead of real people' (Kathleen and James McGinnis, *Parenting for Peace and Justice*).

. . .it is not the fact of difference which is important to grasp, but the ways in which those differences are ranked, given different weighting in society and used as the basis for exploitation and oppression.
Maurice Hobbs, *Better Will Come*

Racism is the outworking of these stereotypes by people who have power: *Racism = Prejudice + Power*. In other words, people who control resources or have decision-making power operate on the basis of the stereotypes, or their prejudices, rather than the truth, or the qualities of an individual. Obvious examples are denying a job to someone because of their ethnic origin, or deciding on educational provision on the basis of supposed racial attributes—the belief that one race is inherently suited to manual work, for example.

But such factors are also used to 'explain' or justify policies or practices that are not so explicitly racist, or to avoid having to face up to issues of justice within society. Why are ethnic minorities disproportionately present in the prison population? And similarly uncommon in the legal profession, and among judges in particular? Why are so many ethnic minority people poor or unemployed? Such situations arise because racism and indirect (or unintentional) racism is still built into society.

While addressing the justice issues that surround race in society, we must also address the propagation of racism in the media, and work to diminish its influence. As long as people of different ethnic groups rarely mix, such prejudices are hard to undermine; a vicious spiral operates in which oppressed groups hold together for comfort and to keep a sense of identity; this minimizes contact with the dominant group and increases the opportunity for prejudice, fear and hatred to grow. The church as an institution sadly is as divided as society.

DISABILITY

There are some 6 million people—more than 1 in 10 of the population—with some physical or mental disability in the UK. The same process of stereotyping and denial of opportunity affects this group too. People with physical disabilities frequently complain that they are seen as a disability to be coped with rather than a human being with abilities. In particular, there is a frequent assumption that a physical disability implies a mental one too. This is particularly acute for people with deafness or cerebral palsy.

Using the definition of racism given earlier, it is clear that people with disabilities suffer from an equivalent process; they are denied access to opportunity solely on the basis of a disability. While physical barriers are the most obvious example, it is frequently reported that it is other people's attitudes that are the greatest impediment. Another equation: *Handicap = Disability + Environment.* A disability is not necessarily a handicap. Being a wheelchair user is OK until you reach the stairs and there is no ramp. Who is handicapped in a cinema when the lights go out? Not a blind person, that's for sure.

Recognition of the skills and potential contribution of people with disabilities is vital; the focus for churches is usually on caring, and on what the disabled person cannot do. Gifted women were not so long ago assumed to have a ministry only to other women or children. Now gifted people with disabilities may similarly be labelled: useful in helping other disabled people, or in dealing with disability issues.

People with learning difficulties, some one million people in the UK, are also a marginalized group, though awareness of this is lower. Assumptions about what they can or cannot do are often based on gross generalizations, ignoring the fact that the vast majority live quite normally within the community. As for other forms of disability, the need is for barriers to involvement in society to be removed; attitudes and communication difficulties are the major areas.

The recent moves from institutional care, with its problems of isolation, institutionalization and lack of care, have created new issues for the church. Community care is seen as cheaper, though partly because of the costs borne by carers and others. The responsibility of churches is to support disabled people and their carers; we are discovering that the community rarely cares as much as it should. Preparing disabled people for life in the community is done to some extent, but not preparing the community for disabled people. Institutional care has encouraged the notion that disability is abnormal, someone else's problem, best ignored and it will go away. The separation has encouraged the forming of stereotypes, as with ethnic minorities.

Disabled children without families are a particularly deprived group.

The essence of good adoption practice is that it is primarily concerned with providing a happy and secure family life for children, rather than babies for would be adopters. The reality is that there are far fewer babies than there are prospective parents in the UK and [yet] the most pressing need is for homes for 'hard-to-place' children.

Christian Childcare Network

Children with disabilities suffer particular problems in participating normally in society; the chance of life in a family is crucial.

MENTAL ILLNESS

One in four people each year suffer some form of mental distress, or illness. Yet too often this is the great taboo, especially in churches. Mental illness is still associated in the minds of many with asylums, where people whose difficulty in coping raises uncomfortable questions about society can instead be forgotten. Huge prejudices still surround the subject, with the feeling that 'Christians shouldn't get depressed' underlying much of our inability to address them.

AGE

Older people are another marginalized group. Far from traditional regard for their experience and stories, today's society feels they have nothing to offer; they are no longer units of production, so they have no value in our economic system. The term 'ageism' has been coined to express negative attitudes to people based on age; simplistic generalizations.

But 'age' (or 'old age') is never an explanation or cause of physical or mental illness or disorder. No diseases only affect people over the age of 65 . . . An older person, like any other, is a person, and a full member of society . . . has his or her own past history, culture and lifelong goals and plans.

Age Concern

Over three million older people live alone; over a million need help to get around. Loneliness, poverty, illness and frustration are the problem; not age. The feeling that there is no one prepared to listen. Apart from being denied the chance to contribute to society, older people are often poor: most in the UK rely on state pension for 75 per cent or more of their income. Yet more than 30 per cent of job adverts in a recent survey included an upper age limit. This is outlawed in the USA and France.

YOUTH

Paradoxically, in what many people see as a youth-dominated culture, there is a significant group of young people at risk. The Frontier Youth Trust identifies those who come from homes where the adults can't cope, reject or fail to understand them. They reject the role models closest to them and find identity in their peer group—solidarity and acceptance. While looking for love, security, freedom, they find failure, unemployment and boredom. They become disillusioned with and mistrust authority; live for the present. They can cope with violence, but not love. They are vulnerable to manipulation.

Their preconceived ideas about church make the contribution of churches problematic. While they experience the world as unloving, insecure and unjust, they feel equally rejected and condemned by society and many Christians. They are unable to respond to patterns of church life and live in the very areas where the church is weakest. Church youth activities are often good at catering for the children of members, but rarely succeed in reaching these young people on the edge of society, who most closely resemble those Christ came to serve.

SINGLENESS

People living alone—single, divorced or widowed of any age—are also marginalized in many churches. The faltering, though still prevailing 'family culture' serves to create the impression that singleness is a deviation from the norm, and, in the context of a society that values sexual experience above all else, the churches in reaction deny single people the opportunity for physical contact of any kind. There is a need not only to affirm singleness as normal and God-given, but also allow the expression of physical affection outside marriage.

▣ SEXUALITY

Of all the marginalized people in society, it is the homosexual community that presents the church with its greatest challenge. For here, questions of individual morality serve to obscure the extent to which homosexual people suffer from much the same processes that we have seen at work elsewhere. Many people, including the majority of Christians, regard the expression of homosexuality as sinful, on the basis of biblical teaching, and appeal to what is 'natural'. But, in common with ethnic minorities, homosexual people also suffer from irrelevant and damaging stereotypes and prejudices.

While greed, promiscuity, gossiping and disobeying parents are equally condemned in scripture, they are seldom seen as impediments to jobs, or full participation in society. This issue has rarely engaged the churches until recently, when the rise of Aids suddenly created the need for a pastoral response to this group.

Christian responses have varied from claiming that Aids is a personal judgment from God upon sinners, to the assertion that Aids is merely a disease like any other. But, alongside these various moral positions, Christians have been at the forefront of social concern for Aids sufferers and HIV carriers, as outcasts from society.

AIDS touches areas of sickness, death and personal behaviour. It brings out prejudice and fear, and people with the disease are often isolated and rejected.

AIDS Care, Education and Training (ACET)

The church does, however, have a problem, as for a long time it has been seen as having a judgmental attitude towards the high risk groups. Now it seeks to reach and counsel them, and trust will take effort to earn.

Apart from 'high risk' groups of people, such as homosexuals, intravenous drug users and haemophiliacs, attention has often focused on 'innocent' children, who can get Aids from sexual abuse, prostitution, and before birth from their mothers. The chances of HIV transmission when pregnant are quite high, (10 per cent is one approximation) and the chances of developing Aids if HIV positive are greater in pregnancy. This raises the thorny issue of abortion, especially as mothers and babies at risk tend to come from already vulnerable and unsupported groups.

All in all, it seems that marginalized groups of one kind or another comprise a large proportion of society! For the churches, there are two fundamental issues to address: to what extent does the church prevent the full involvement of these people, and their full expression? And what role can the church play in establishing a just and caring society, reflecting the hope that we hold?

GROUP WORK

All Christian communities live among marginalized people; most include several of the groups discussed in the introduction. But, because they are marginalized, their experience and skills are rarely given expression in church life. This is a good time to begin. Your own situation is unique—you may have representatives of marginalized groups within your own ranks; listening to their views and experience (without seeking to explain them away) may be the most useful way to begin. If not, consider inviting someone from the wider church or neighbourhood in to speak to your group and help you to decide how you may wish to respond to the problem of marginalization.

All people are equally loved by God; Christ died even for those hostile to him. The problem is, human society undervalues some, pushing them to the fringes. To our shame, so does the church.

A SUGGESTED FORMAT

It may be useful for all group members to read the introduction to this section, perhaps before you meet, so that you all have a common starting point. 'Who are the marginalized?' is a way to prioritize areas of concern and may help to clarify marginalization in your situation, in general terms. 'The Bible and marginalized groups' explores some of the general principles that emerge from the Bible. The remaining sections raise issues of concern to specific groups of people. Select elements from these sections according to your own priorities.

WHO ARE THE MARGINALIZED?

In small groups, mark four concentric rings on a large sheet of paper: the church, our families, our neighbourhoods, the wider community. Note down the marginalized groups you are aware of in these areas. Take time for this; some groups are almost invisible. Come together and decide which groups are particularly relevant to the situation your group finds itself in. How do you decide this?

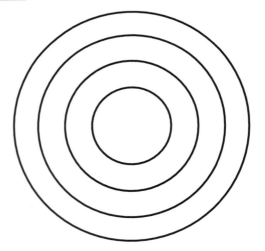

What contact do you have with people from these groups? What determines the nature of this contact? What images do you have of them? Are these real? How do you get these impressions? How could you make more contact with them?

Are there people from any of these marginalized groups who take part in the life of the church? Do any hold positions of responsibility? If not, what prevents this? What 'conditions of entry' may exclude them? What barriers may prevent them from participating fully? Getting there, getting in, getting involved, getting noticed.

THE BIBLE AND MARGINALIZED GROUPS

As an exclusive race, the Jewish people in biblical times had a problem with marginalization, too. The Old Testament has specific laws to ensure that vulnerable groups had access to the resources they needed. What groups of people can you identify from the Bible who were pushed to the edge, disregarded or despised?

Isaiah 53; 1 Corinthians 1:26–31. How does this reflect on society's preoccupation with beauty, health and intelligence?

1 Corinthians 12:12–31. Do we take this seriously when it comes to disabled, old, young or other marginalized people?
Genesis 3:14–19; Romans 8:18–22. Some people blame disability on sin and the fall. Just whose sin is the cause of marginalization?
Galatians 6:1–5. How does the church respond to this in the case of those caring for disabled, mentally ill or elderly people?
James 2:1–13. How does the church measure up with respect to the different groups of people discussed in the introduction?
Luke 5:12–13, 9:40–48; John 4:4–9, 27. How do we respond to the example of Jesus, in relation to the different groups discussed?

PEOPLE WITH DISABILITIES

Read these quotations. Individually pick out the one that makes most impact on you. Come together and share why.

The question is not, 'What role should disabled people play in the church?' but, 'Do we allow disability to handicap people's role in the church?'

Congregations just don't want to know, because this to them would be a very negative part of life . . .

I know one thing that should never, never be said: that 'it is God's will'. If you truly believe in God's love, how could you think he could deliberately make a baby with any kind of disability?

When we deny mentally and physically disabled people the opportunity to contribute to society, we deny the fact that they are made in the image of the creative God.

Disability is thankfully no longer seen as punishment for sin, but handicap stands as a judgment upon society.

In small groups, discuss your own attitudes to disability; in what way do you contribute towards turning disabilities into handicaps? Review this in the larger group. How could you help the church to reconsider its attitudes towards disabled people?

Review the 'Action' guide and consider what you might do to improve the scope within the church and society for disabled people to contribute.

PEOPLE OF DIFFERENT ETHNIC BACKGROUNDS

You have to leave parts of you at the door. Things like the way you speak, the ways that you relate to each other... they are regarded as just not meaningful... by the white leadership. Our experiences have not been given any value at all.

When racism is 'institutionalised' it often falls to quite ordinary people—some...committed Christians—to, operate 'the system', conscientiously following 'rule books' and traditional procedures, with integrity.

[In a survey of Birmingham Anglican churches]... of the 89 churches with mixed congregations, 47 had no black members on the PCC... Of the 13 youth leaders, 2 were black... On the diocesan synod, 2 members were black out of 135 lay representatives.

In our church, leaders are recognized on the basis of ability and willingness to get involved; we have no need for an equal opportunities policy.

... we had the idea. We raised the money, designed the engine and the carriages, decided where the line should run. Then we got up steam ... and invited our black fellow Christians on board as passengers. Then we're surprised that they didn't buy the ticket.

The Church should not simply reflect the divisions and distancing present in its social context ... If the gospel has truly brought reconciliation ... then the local church should demonstrate the reality of this theological truth in practical terms to the community.

Eddie Gibbs, I Believe in Church Growth

List some prejudiced attitudes that you hold, and discuss ways in which you could challenge them. How could you put yourself in a situation which might assist change? What past experiences have changed your views of other ethnic groups? Prejudice is difficult to recognize in oneself, and even more difficult to admit to. Honesty and imagination are essential.

Together list ways in which stereotyped images and prejudiced attitudes are promoted in society. Discuss ways in which you could counter their influence.

What ethnic minority groups are represented in your neighbourhood? To what extent do people from these groups have leadership roles? How does the church compare?

Together list some of the factors that may discourage shared leadership.

Review the 'Action' guide and consider what you might do to improve the church and society as environments for people from ethnic minorities.

OLDER PEOPLE

Follow the section on 'Disabled people', but with older people in mind. What are the parallels between age and disability? How do we make age a handicap in society?

Review the 'Action' guide and consider what you might do to improve the scope within the church and society for older people to contribute.

YOUNG PEOPLE

Think individually, and then discuss: what impressions come to mind when thinking of young people in the city or on the large housing estate? Are the images real or stereotyped? Which denote good news? bad news? How do the bad and good news come about?

How do young people in these areas view the church? Why? What contact do you have with young people? From other backgrounds? What determines the nature of this contact?

Jobs: what is like for young people to get jobs? Do you know anyone finding it difficult? What is the typical pay like?

Homes: where can a single person stay? Do you know of anyone sleeping rough? What could you do to help?

The church has failed: to recognise this group; to change its attitude towards them; to go out to them; to help them respond; to respect them as people to whom Christ primarily ministered.

Work with young people on the margins is like foreign mission work.

Youth work is not to keep kids off the streets . . . it's the degree to which you are willing to share their lives. The closer you get . . . the greater the possibility of hurt, rejection, abuse and crucifixion.

How do you react to these statements? What kind of support might youth workers need? Where can they get it? How involved is the church in any youth work it officially sanctions? How could it better support such work? How could such work better reach marginalized young people? How could you begin to identify their needs?

Review the 'Action' guide and consider what you might do to improve the scope within the church and society for young people to contribute.

SINGLE PEOPLE

If your group has single members who feel able to contribute to a discussion, spend some time listening to their view of the church as a family and ways it could work better. Discuss how individuals and church

bodies could help this process.

If not, why not invite a group from a church body to which singles do belong? They will need briefing beforehand and may want to review this section.

MENTALLY ILL PEOPLE

Have any members of your group suffered from mental illness or distress? If so, how was this handled within the church; what support was available? What attitudes and fears surround

mental illness within the church? How does this differ from attitudes you are aware of in the wider community?

HOMOSEXUAL PEOPLE

One major reason for Christian concern for homosexuality is the arrival of Aids in the population, but here we look at the issue of marginalization.

Read and discuss these quotes:

A clear distinction can be made between sexual orientation and sexual practice.

How can anything be a sin when so much love is involved?

I am only sixteen, but I am as sure as I can be that I am a lesbian. I am not happy about this because I know that in the eyes of God I am a sinner ... Will I go to hell, or will it make any difference if I marry, like other girls?

I got HIV from my first boyfriend—I was 17.

People with Aids should not be allowed to live in the community.

The worst thing about having Aids is the way people treat me.

I've lost my job, and my family and friends have started ignoring me, but Aids is only another illness.

Discuss this true story:

A man was tested for HIV without his knowledge during an operation. The surgeon informed his doctor by letter that he was positive. When he visited his doctor later, the receptionist mentioned the letter to a colleague and was overheard by a waiting patient. That night, the man's house was burned down.

ACTION ON MARGINALIZATION

GENERAL POINTS

This section assumes that you have identified a group of marginalized people in your local community that you think the church could do more to support in their determination to play a full part in society. Your precise course of action will depend on your priorities, and specific sources of help are listed in the 'Resources' section. Here we look in general terms at the actions you might become involved in.

One theme repeated again and again by those representing marginalized groups is that other people's attitudes are the greatest problem. Even when we wish to help, it is all too easy to fall into the trap of working for rather than with the people really involved. This is particularly the case with older people and those with disabilities, but applies to other groups too. The principle has to be one of empowerment, otherwise whatever you do may only address the symptoms rather than the causes of marginalization.

Having said that, many church groups will not have a representative from any of the groups discussed with whom to consult as a matter of course. One possible solution is to try out any new initiative as a pilot scheme, in which one person gets involved in main activities to blaze the trail for others. You will need to find someone likely to express their views frankly! Any candidates from within the church?

You will need to seek help and advice, by involving people and organizations representing or working with the groups you wish to work with, for mutual help and support. Have you talked to marginalized people or their advocates, or are you basing your initiatives on what you *think* is needed? The 'Resources' section includes the addresses of organizations with a local presence. Do contact them to find out what is going on in your area before taking any action.

The 'Resources' section refers to a number of study and action resources specific to certain issues. To learn more about the subject, do consider some further study.

Be prepared to make time to develop your programme of action, and for communication with the people you hope to serve. Make a plan and a timetable; establish a working party and an agreed aim.

ACTION IN THE HOME

The home is potentially a huge resource, and it is also the place where the attitudes of the coming generation are formed. Possible actions concentrate on these two areas.

We all pick up messages from the media, and the television is the most powerful at creating images. Unfortunately, it is also viewed uncritically; we usually see it as a diversion and let its imagery flow around us without challenge. A first stage in claiming independence is to carry out a survey in order to become aware of the hidden and perhaps unintended messages that come across.

For your (and/or your children's) favourite programmes

Check for the image given of marginalized groups, if there are any. Are they the main characters, or merely supporting roles? Are they shown as 'important' in the community; in any leadership role? Are they there purely to allow the dominant characters to develop their role? Are they shown as anything more than their 'label' or stereotype (disabled, old, youth, mentally ill)?

Adverts, news, documentaries etc

List the major ones you remember; are there any marginalized groups featured?

Other media

When reading books for yourself or children, look for representatives of marginalized groups in the same way. Are they there at all? Are they main characters? Are they stereotypes? Look for children's books that provide a counterbalance to the prevailing images of marginalized groups. Visual images in books are also important.

Other input at home includes the various friends and visitors who come, the visits and contacts you make. Do these reflect the real society we have, or are marginalized groups under-represented? Do the 'professionals' (such as doctors, teachers) you see represent ethnic minority or other groups in the community? Work with local organizations representing marginalized groups may well change the 'balance' of the people you meet and who visit your home.

A more radical approach is to change the population of your home on a temporary or permanent basis. Children with special needs are 'difficult to place' yet have great need of secure home backgrounds. Fostering and respite care of such children is a hugely beneficial way to use the resources of your home. Adoption is a longer term commitment, but even more valuable. See the relevant agencies in the 'Resources' list. Some agencies also promote the fostering of elderly people and adults with mental disabilities, as a break from institutional care.

Even our patterns of consumption at home can be an influence on the social environment of some marginalized groups of people. As employers, the companies we buy from have varying records on the employment of disabled people, older people and ethnic minorities. By buying from companies with a more positive approach, any household can 'vote' for a better working life. New Consumer's *Shopping for a Better World* is the shopping guide with all the information. See the address list in the Introduction, or look in your book shop.

WORK/SCHOOL

If you work outside the home, then an important avenue for action is to find out about the policies of your employer towards the employment of ethnic minorities, older people and disabled people. Does it discriminate against older people in candidate selection? Does it have any affirmative policies to ensure that people from ethnic minorities have opportunities for employment and promotion? Has it introduced facilities and access arrangements for disabled people? Are there any ethnic minority senior staff or directors? One doesn't need to rock the boat excessively to draw to the attention of senior managers the need for such policies, and the concern of existing staff.

Schools are also employers, of course, and parents, through the governing body, have every right to query employment policies in the same way as other consumers. But schools also offer an important environment in which children take on values and attitudes. The key question is, does the broad curriculum represent any marginal perspectives? Does the school have a policy on racism with regard to the curriculum and resource materials, for example? Is there any contact with marginalized communities, for example, with special schools in a twinning arrangement? Does the school make use of visiting 'experts' who also come from marginalized groups, in order to counteract stereotyped negative images? Does the school population reflect the community as a whole? If not, why not?

CHURCH

The same question can be asked, with more force, of the church. How mixed is it? If there is a problem, then the issues of access and participation need to be addressed. A key issue is that of building links between the church and the various organizations representing and working with marginalized groups (and those who care for people with disabilities). These links are not primarily to find out what the church can do for the different groups, but to find out what barriers prevent people getting involved—listening rather than acting, at first.

Church Action on Disability have a good access audit, with disabled people in mind (see 'Resources'). This looks at physical and attitudinal barriers to entry and active participation. Many of the questions are relevant to other groups.

The overall aim of all these efforts should be an integrated congregation, not an increase in attendance at services by one group at the expense of another; that may well lead to an apartheid system whereby different groups attend special services, or different groups sit in different places.

In the case of ethnic minority communities, those with a high proportion of Christians will often have developed their own churches, following their own style of worship and church life. While, in the long term, integration of worship may be desirable, links between 'black-led' churches and local indigenous congregations are a possibility. The Evangelical Alliance has some experience of this, and will be worth contacting.

Many churches have attached youth work, be it a youth club for the children of members, or an open youth centre. As suggested above, these efforts may not reach marginalized, or 'frontier', youth, and those youth workers who are in touch may lack understanding church support. Frontier Youth Trust suggests a number of strategies: adopt a youth worker—ask her/him to share ideas with you about their work and suggest how you might help; 'adopt' a youth club that serves the needs of these people, or help in one; start something locally, if nothing else meets the need. FYT can help.

COMMUNITY

It is the church serving the wider community that is most likely to be the focus of effort. This work operates at a number of levels.

Caring, especially for disabled people, is the most obvious: how can you help, in real life, to overcome barriers, recover a sense of community, gain access to resources and the practical necessities of life? Day centres, transport, lunch clubs, pop-ins, day and evening classes, carer support, counselling and holidays can all help to overcome isolation. Those with physical disabilities may need hospital aftercare, advice and care services, keep-fit sessions. Practical help, such as gardening, decorating, insulation, repairs, home safety, can help meet social as well as physical needs. Likewise, voluntary involvement in residential care can supply the social contact that is needed.

One group of people often marginalized by circumstances is those who care for physically or mentally disabled people, or frail older people. Sharing the caring role with the families can be a real lifeline. Social services, as well as local voluntary organizations, are sources of information here. Church buildings may well provide a home for meetings, day centres, and other activities outlined, if no homes already exist. In the first instance, involvement is likely to be more efficient if done in the context of existing voluntary organizations, where they are already active. There is inevitably a learning phase, and history is littered with well-meaning projects that achieved little because people did not learn first.

But involvement at this level, while important and under-resourced, may only patch up the wounds, not deal with the deeper problem. More support implies more listening.

Marginalized groups, by definition, often find difficulty in getting their message, their perspective, across to those responsible for resource allocation. Involvement with such groups may well yield opportunities for advocacy: based on contacts with disabled people, using the resources of the church to lobby for access to facilities and other resources in the local community.

NATION/WORLD

At this level, action is very much of the lobbying kind. Resource decisions are increasingly centralized and legislative change is often the way to achieve some of the targets you may have. Writing to MPs, MEPs and newspapers may seem almost hackneyed now, but very few people do it. Similarly, writing to companies about their employment policies, and the media about their portrayal of marginalized groups can be very effective. Everyone knows that behind every letter are a hundred people with the same views.

What to write about is beyond the scope of this guide, of course, but any living involvement with marginalized people will raise a host of issues that should motivate action at this level. The key, as outlined in the Introduction, is the question 'Why?' Why are some disablement benefits not available to people over sixty-five? Why are more ethnic minorities unemployed? Why are there no ramps into the civic centre? Who decides?

Joining the organizations in the 'Resources' guide will be a source of up-to-date issues of concern, and many of them seek to encourage supporters to make their voices heard. Why not make part of the life of the group to encourage each other to write letters—and to pray about the same issue? We can petition God and those in authority together.

▇ RESOURCES

ORGANIZATIONS

Aids Care, Education and Training, ACET
Aims to provide practical care and support to men, women and children with Aids, irrespective of race, religion, lifestyle, sexual orientation or any other factor; to reduce new infections by educating young people; to equip the church to make an effective Christian response to Aids, respecting the historic teachings of the church and providing unconditional care. Runs ACET-link, a church link scheme, raising awareness and funds, as well as prayer support. ACET volunteers provide transport, daysit, nightsit, do housework, cook, collect prescriptions, befriend. They work as part of homecare system with doctors and nurses, do education work in schools, and work in Africa.

Age Concern Bernard Sunley House, Pitcairn Road, Mitcham, Surrey CR4 3LL. Aims to promote well-being, fulfilment and happiness of older people. Runs day centres, lunch clubs, pop-ins, transport services, carer support, counselling, holidays, classes. Provides hospital aftercare, advice and care services, keep-fit sessions. Practical help: gardening, decorating, insulation, repairs, home safety. Local groups (over 250,000 volunteers). Nationally it advises agencies and campaigns with and on behalf of older people. Provides a range of books on financial and health matters, coping with loneliness, caring for confused elderly people, old age abuse, discrimination and other issues.

A Cause for Concern (Christian concern for mentally handicapped people). 118b Oxford Road, Reading, RG1 7NG. Runs homes for mentally handicapped people, meeting the need created by the fact that many more mentally handicapped children are outliving their parents. Also develops materials for churches to get involved with mentally handicapped people in their communities—Causeway.

Help the Aged Provides transport, housing and information. Publishes advice leaflets on financial, safety and health issues. Local groups involved in fundraising. Works internationally via HelpAge International.

Church Action on Disability (CHAD) Charisma Cottage, Drewsteignton, Exeter EX6 6QR. Offers an exhibition for display, mail order books, voluntary contacts, a magazine. Basis: all people should be able to participate in God's work, but people with disabilities are often excluded. Committed to increasing acceptance, understanding and participation.

The PHAB Christian Fellowship PHAB Club Services Unit, Bushland Road, Weston Favell, Northampton. A forum for social contact between physically disabled and able-bodied people.

Christian Impact Stimulates Christians to think and act effectively on contemporary social, cultural and spiritual issues within a biblical framework. Runs courses, publishes study materials and books, and has a local group network.

Christians Against Racism and Fascism
1 Brock Place, Devons Road, London E3.

Evangelical Christians for Racial Justice
12 Bell Barn Shopping Centre, Cregoe Street, Birmingham B15 2DZ. Exists to challenge racism in Britain, raise awareness in the churches, encourage joint action for peace and justice and provide information and resources to churches.

Frontier Youth Trust 130 City Road, London EC1V 2NJ. A network of and for people working with young people at risk, on the 'margins' of society; the inner city, large housing estates or isolated rural areas. It offers support, training, advice and opportunities for theological reflection.

MIND 22 Harley Street, London W1N 2ED. Works for a better life for and campaigns on behalf of people suffering from mental illness. It stresses the needs of oppressed groups: ethnic minorities, women. Local associations are involved in counselling, relatives' support schemes, employment and housing projects, drop-in centres, drug withdrawal workshops. Charity shops too. Publishes briefings, books and leaflets on all aspects of mental health, from legal to advice work, from special problems of ethnic minorities to help for carers.

Terrence Higgins Trust 52–54 Grays Inn Road, London WC1X 8JU. Help and support for those with HIV and Aids.

ACTION/DISCUSSION MATERIAL

CHAD Study Pack: £6 plus 75p p. and p.

CHAD Access audit for churches: £1. Scope of the audit: barriers to entry and movement; barriers to participation in meetings; barriers to participation in ministry/service. From CHAD.

CHAD Access Pack: £5 plus 60p p. and p. A very practical guide. Ways to plan for the changes needed to enable access; a planner from the Centre for Accessible Environments; information about assisting wheelchair users, large print Bibles, induction loop systems, etc.

Christian Impact Study Series 'AIDS', 'Mental handicap'. Each is a selection of booklets, discussion material and often a cassette tape, £5. Christian Impact Publications, 79 Maid Marian Way, Nottingham NG1 6AE.

ECRJ Study Pack, 'New Humanity', £5 from ECRJ (address p. 107).

__Mission and Young People at Risk__ an Frontier Youth Trust Workbook, £3.20. The why, where and how for churches wanting to improve their service to young people at risk. Very detailed and practical, with references to other organizations' resources.

Grove booklets from Grove Books, Bramcote, Notts, NG9 3DS. 'A Place in the Family: The single person in the local church'; 'New Approaches to Ministry With Older People', £1.75. 'AIDS: A Christian Response', £1.95.

Shaftesbury Society Community Involvement Pack, £19.95 plus £3 p. and p.

__The Local Church and Mental Handicap__ a DIY pack from Scripture Union.

__One Door Shuts__ a video about work with young people on the edges of society. With discussion notes. Free loan from Frontier Youth Trust.

CONSUMER CULTURE 7

First, a little quiz. What do Shredded Wheat, Terry's Chocolate Orange, Maxwell House coffee, Dairylea cheese, Instant Whip, Marlboro cigarettes and Branston Pickle all have in common?

Together with another over six hundred other brands they are owned by one or other of the world's two largest food companies, Swiss-owned Nestlé and American-owned Philip Morris. These companies are so big that their combined turnover is larger than the gross national income of more than 170 of the world's nations. Put it another way, what was paid for their products last year was equal to the gross national product of Austria, or enough to give a present of more than £10 to every woman, man and child on earth. And how did these companies get so big? The answer is simple: we helped them.

In the First World we are still in the middle of a consumer revolution. Its present and most dramatic phase started about 1960. If we go back about a hundred years, as a nation of about 30 million people we were spending just over £1 billion on goods and services. By 1960 the 51 million of us were spending around £30 billion, but in 1993 we spent over £400 billion. Even allowing for inflation and a slight increase in population we are massively better off in material terms than we were thirty years ago.

But something even more dramatic has happened in the last hundred years. In 1893 we spent nearly all our money through tens of thousands of small businesses. In 1993 about half of what you spend will be on the goods and services provided by fewer than 250 companies. Look in your local town centre or shopping mall and you will see names that appear nearly everywhere in Britain. While we have more choice than ever before about what we buy, we have less and less choice about where we buy it. Let's go back to all this money we spend as consumers. It's more than two hundred times what we give to charity. If the average person were to make a slight change in how they shop to the benefit of social and environmental issues it could have more impact that all the money they give away. And why should they? For the reasons that we do anything that isn't self-interested— because we care about others, because we are trying to love our neighbours as ourselves. Does this mean that the whole idea of a sustainable lifestyle, of living more simply, cutting back or changing to those goods and services which are going to build a better world runs against the whole tide of consumerism? Putting others first is hardly a good slogan to sell products.

We may not have a choice. We are increasingly faced with problems that are going to affect all us, rich or poor, like it or not. The issues are already with us: the thinning of the ozone layer, global warming, pollution and rain-forest depletion, population growth, desertification, famine, Aids, Third World and personal debt, the first dramatic and tragic instance of a war over resources in the Gulf, and the start of numerous ethnic and territorial wars that we seem powerless to prevent or stop. Consumerism seems to have done a lot for the affluent but it is clearly is not enough for the planet as a whole. What is ironic is that we have successfully exported the concept of an ever-growing personal prosperity, the principle of 'I shop therefore I am', just as it is being questioned at its deepest level. More and more people are asking, 'Can we go on like this . . . is it sustainable . . . is not the whole system flawed and ultimately self-destructive?'

The blunt answer is that we cannot go on like this, but can we somehow reform the very idea of consumerism. The world of marketing has traditionally argued that there are two kinds of benefit for the consumer when they purchase something. The function benefit, what the product actually does, and the psychological benefit, what the product says about you. Most advertising concentrates on this last aspect and applies whether the product is detergent, a car or a package holiday. The big question is whether a third benefit can emerge, the idea of social investment, when people will ask, 'When I spend money in this way, what am I doing for my true well-being or the well-being of others and future generations?'

We need to think carefully through our values as consumers. These values may involve concern about exploitation of resources, pollution of the environment, cruelty to animals, and the development of human beings as whole, free, creative people. They might be about peace and justice, about the rights and opportunities of minorities, about secrecy, about size, about power, about manipulators who turn wants into needs while ignoring the real needs of the poor and powerless. Many of these values are implicit in the Gospels; there is a people-centredness about them that Christians must respond to. The public are beginning to appreciate that the vital issues of the coming decades will revolve around the nature of global consumption and distribution. Fundamental choices will have to be made about lifestyle, patterns of production and consumer priorities. Planet-sustaining decisions must be based on extensive and wide-ranging information about the nature of our consumer society and those who service it.

Does our spending create a better world, or are we supporting companies that want to make profits whatever the social or moral costs? Is our leisure being created for us by those companies; are we taking in the message to spend, acquire, consume? Are we still being taken in by the message that only by showing my purchasing capacity can I prove myself as a real person? Do we nod sagely when politicians promise us ever-expanding affluence? All these attitudes need to be questioned; we need to become disturbed and make others share our unease about what is going on in our society. It sounds uncomfortable, but it's uncomfortable for the people starving in the Sudan, it's uncomfortable for the Indians in the Amazon rainforest seeing their world burn around them, it's uncomfortable for the homeless on the streets of our big cities. All these people are being crushed and distorted by the uncaring power of our global economic juggernaut, which, as juggernauts have a tendency to do, shows every sign of running out of control. Its not too late, but to change its course we need to change our own.

Tourism concern

This theme finds one of its most uncomfortable forms of expression in the influence of tourism on Third World cultures. For many countries, tourism seems an ideal earner: one of the few ways you can sell your assets (weather, beaches, exotic culture . . .) and still keep them to sell again. But life is never that simple, of course. At its simplest, tourism erodes the very environment it relies on: beaches become hotels, seas become polluted. But the social costs of tourism can be as serious, as the influence of extremes of wealth and poverty show the effects of consumer culture in the raw.

The easy (if temporary) wealth of the tourist means that everything is for sale, and the symbols and rituals that defined a culture are now re-produced for sale (or even faked). Human contact becomes subjugated to human contract as locals are seen as servants (or even beggars) rather than hosts, and tourists are easy-money punters rather than guests. The particular horrors of sex tourism are mirrored, if at a less shocking level, in a hundred and one less-than-human contacts made yearly in the name of getting away from it all.

While we tend to blame consumers for everything from global resource depletion to recession (we are not 'confident' enough!) we are of course all consumers, as well as citizens, voters, newspaper readers, children, parents ... Compartmentalizing us as consumers, whose interests are met by 'efficient' agriculture, or low raw materials prices, or new roads or free market competition or whatever, in effect undervalues our role as citizens (or human beings) where justice, community, loyalty, care, beauty and so forth are probably even more important. The move to a new kind of consumerism begun by the green consumer movement underlies this: we need to assert that we (consumers/citizens/parents/Christians/people/friends etc ...) are not to be slaves to the market, to economic 'realities', but vice versa.

If British coal is more 'expensive'; if sustainable agriculture is 'uneconomic'; if fair prices for Third World goods are 'unrealistic', then we need a new economics that works for us and allows us to pursue these deeper goals. We need to bring into the equation all the costs involved in producing goods—the social costs of exploitation or redundancy, the environmental costs of pollution, the costs to be borne by our children of resource depletion—and then we can decide what is truly *economic*. And we will find that it is also environmentally sustainable, socially just and supportive of true community.

But, looking around us at the real world, it seems that such thinking has made little impact yet. The 1980s, now remembered as the decade of greed, was really memorable as the time in which society at large began to realize what it loses when the consumer is king (or queen). One event of the last three years which puts the issue into focus was the Lloyd's insurance 'disaster'. Because of heavy insurance losses at this time, people who had become 'names'—underwriting losses with their own wealth—stood to lose far more than they had invested. What was striking was the complete acceptance (by the media at least) of the greed motive.

'There was nothing ethically wrong in their behaviour—the pursuit of money is a lust like any other. In reality, what most of them wanted was huge profits for sitting on their hands while others took the risks.' (*The Guardian*, 25 June 1992)

'Names' accepted the idea of unlimited liability in pursuit of the huge potential profits available while doing no work. The money used to underwrite insurance was at the same time available for investment, thus earning a double return. While there is the need to be concerned about the individual hardship that resulted, it should properly be seen not as undeserved suffering, but as the inevitable consequence of greed.

Working out how such values are developed and propagated in society is no mean task, as each of us is exposed to a huge range of influences. But the mass media are undoubtedly a major influence, not just because they are powerful means of communication, but because of their nature.

The modern mass media in Britain now perform many of the integrative functions of the Church in the middle ages. Like the medieval church, the media link together different groups and provide a shared experience that promotes collective values that bind people closer together ...
James Curran, *Culture, Society and the Media*

It is interesting to speculate whether, in the words of Marx, the media have also become the opium of the people! As an example of the media's power to change thought patterns, when Michelle in *EastEnders* decided against an abortion, many doctors reported other pregnant teenagers changing their minds, too.

THE MEDIA AND OUR VALUES

The mass media, and television and newspapers are the key ones, are increasingly the means by which people understand the world, and hence develop their value systems. But the same media that bring us into community with the starving in Somalia also bring us adverts to create our wants and entertainments to dull our concerns. More deeply, the media hold a distorting mirror up to society, creating the danger of distorted values.

Essentially TV is an image—it tells a story—but it is commonly understood to be the truth. We perceive the truth through a multiplicity of partial images, while TV appears to claim that it is the one true image—after all it is real people we see on the screen.

In pursuit of a powerful story, news editors and reporters tend to dramatize situations, create an image of conflict and polarize a situation where detailed negotiation behind the scenes is going on. Negotiation often cannot be reported and therefore, as far as TV is concerned, does not happen. People are seen as their image, not as real people (Lady Thatcher and Arthur Scargill are classic examples). This is made more important by the fact that the audience—the people—see this image as truth, and the image then *becomes* the reality. Many politicians, aware of the importance of media image, use this fact to pressurize others; they play a dual role—one on TV, the other round the table. The media have begun not merely to report and analyze, but to influence. While the media polarize situations so that middle ground appears not to exist (you must believe this or that), the Christian position of reconciliation (whatever side you are on) is undermined. It looks too weak for good television, and perhaps too complex to put across in the thirty seconds allowed for analysis. In politics especially, the fact that television is essentially visual has a distorting influence. Politics must be understood and analyzed intellectually. TV is 'a crude medium which strikes at the emotions rather than the intellect' (Robin Day). Consider the TV role in portraying Ethiopia, Somalia or Bosnia: it stirs people but achieves less real understanding of why problems happen and how we can address them or prevent them; that message has taken much longer to develop.

The scope for manipulation is high when you can mobilize emotional responses and critical responses are temporarily disengaged. An example might be the American TV evangelist Jimmy Bakker or the Live Aid event; in both cases, people parted with large sums of money without any real understanding of how the money was to be used, and little awareness of the need for accountability. Both manipulated the emotions; but in one case, this was done in a 'good' cause by people with integrity.

Advertising is a particular aspect of the media for consideration in this section. Mike Starkey, in *Born to Shop*, sees adverts as . . .

. . . icons of Western consumer society. A icon is a form of art which embodies something of the dreams and ideals of the age . . . In medieval Europe icons of the Virgin and child inspired the faithful to devotion . . .

But what is the message of our icons?

. . . that consumption is the answer to a range of basic human questions . . . Consumer advertising channels all our desires for a better world towards striving for consumer goods and personal prosperity.

However, TV can be good, too: it has brought art into people's homes in a way that libraries never managed; it has allowed people on a low income access to culture otherwise denied them, even Open University. As a powerful medium, it can encourage positive values and 'make goodness interesting' when used well, but the demands to attract a mass audience create a difficult mix of motives. Here advertising has an increasing influence, which brings us full circle. The need to attract viewers relates not to the need to be popular, so much as the need to attract advertising revenue. The pressure to get rid of the *Highway* religious slot, despite its 7–8 million viewers, came because, being primarily over forty-five and in socio-economic groups C2, D and E, they are not very attractive to advertisers.

The logical consequence of this, and the opening up of the airwaves to satellite channels dependent on advertising, is that people not attractive to advertisers will have no programmes made for them. Children, old people, ethnic minorities, religious groups. Already satellite children's programmes are primarily designed to promote toys. The worst scenario is chilling, but public concern is there and the church is making its views known.

So the equation of consumer culture is complete: we over-consume, because the culture we have created values possession above all else; and we propagate our culture through media whose agenda is set by advertisers.

If the media are becoming the most significant means by which society is integrated and propagates its values, where does that leave God? Is he part of the consumer society? Does he, as Tom Sine put it, really help us find parking places when there are children starving in Ethiopia? As Christians, we have borrowed the life-goals of the society in which we live— the pursuit of happiness.

In fact, it would be difficult to find a goal for human life that is more antithetical to everything Jesus represented. Jesus called his followers not to seek life, but to lose life . . . Instead of serving God, we expect him to serve us . . . indulge our desires, spare us inconvenience, and ensure our success in every venture. This unfortunate reversal is most apparent in prayer meetings where petitions are focused almost exclusively on the needs, desires and ambitions of those present . . . We have actually come to believe that happiness has something to do with how much we accumulate.

E. F. Schumacher, in *The Economics of Conservation*, brings us back to a recurring theme of this section: conservation

. . . challenges the 'sacred cow' of the modern world, namely the prevailing religion of economics which sees the primary meaning and purpose of human life in the limitless expansion of every man's needs, that is to say, his craving for more and more material satisfaction . . . We cannot continue to deify economic progress in purely quantitative terms . . . if it is not to lead to disaster it must be progress according to a new pattern inspired by a profound understanding of, and a deep reverence for, our natural environment which is not man-made but God-given.

Hans Kung puts it another, and equally forceful, way.

Despite all progress, our efficiency-oriented and consumer society is increasingly entangled in contradictions. Supported by an economic theory extolled on all sides, the slogan runs: increase production so that we can increase consumption, so that production does not break down but expands. In this way, the level of demand is always kept above the level of supply: through advertising, models and bellwethers of consumption. Wants continue to increase. New needs are created as soon as the old are satisfied. Luxury goods are classified as necessary consumer goods, in order to make way for new luxury goods. The targets of our own living standards are raised with the improvement of the supply situation. There is now a dynamic expectation of prosperity and a satisfying life. The surprising result is that, with constantly increasing real income, the average citizen feels that he is really living at a minimum of existence.

But the Christian message can make something clear which is apparently not envisaged at all either in the economic theory or in the practical scale of values ... replacement of the compulsion to consume by freedom in regard to consumption. In the light of Jesus Christ it also makes sense not to be always striving, not always to be trying to have everything; not to be governed by the laws of prestige and competition; not to take part in the cult of abundance; but even with children to exercise the freedom to renounce consumption. This is 'poverty in spirit' as inward freedom from possessions: contented unpretentiousness and confident unconcernedness as a basic attitude.

Mike Starkey believes that

...people in the West do 'need' a lot of their consumer gimmickry to hold onto a sense of identity. The answer is less to tell people to throw away the trash than to teach people to root an identity in more valuable sources, such as family, community, faith and a different set of values.

The key issue for Christians is not merely to propagate these values through society, but to develop them in ourselves and our children; we too are creatures of our time. In *Parenting for Peace and Justice*, Kathleen and James McGinnis identify these 'Goals in stewardship':

◆ Greater concern for life—and people—rather than things

◆ Relationships—good times base on people rather than things

◆ Self-reliance—less dependence on possessions and money for happiness and security means greater reliance on own insights and abilities

◆ Personal growth—greater awareness of our own motivations and unconscious patterns of life.

We Western Christians tend to be so caught up in our timetables, our activities, our projects and our efforts to preserve our place at the party, that we have no time left over for what was one of the central preoccupations of Jesus' life—celebrating his relationships with other people. Our brothers and sisters in the Third World have much to teach us about how to put aside our quest for acquiring and possessing, and simply to relish the people around us.

Tom Sine

We believe Christ calls us to dissent from our present lifestyles and make a radical break from the patterns of over-indulgence, consumerism and reckless waste. We are called individually and ecclesiastically to choose a lifestyle which more nearly reflects the simplicity of Jesus' life and allows us to identify with the poor and powerless throughout the earth. Such an altered lifestyle enables us to reconsider what we truly value in life, how we measure success, where we live, what we eat, how we use energy, how we invest our lives and resources, and where and how we travel. In short, we are challenged to live more simply that all may simply live.

US Presbyterian church, 1979

GROUP WORK

One of the difficulties inherent in discussing culture, be it consumer culture or otherwise, is that our own is invisible. As we only realize what 'Britishness' is when we travel, we find it difficult to identify our own culture until we experience another. As Christians, we have an alternative model (or perhaps several) as we look at the Bible and at the values that God intends his people to share. However, there is the tendency to interpret even this in the light of our own culture, which has for centuries absorbed some of the symbols of Christianity, and we too easily confuse the two.

In the light of this, it is important to avoid the temptation to reject alternative views too quickly; they should be measured against the Bible rather than the *Daily Mail* or *The Guardian*. It would also be useful, if a counsel of perfection, to have input from somebody brought up in a different culture. Christianity interpreted in poor communities of the 'Third World' has some tough and important questions to ask of ours. You may like to review some of the material in the section on poverty as a way of clearing away some of our cultural debris before you start.

A SUGGESTED FORMAT

Since consumerism is so much a part of our culture, it is good to start with the Bible and review the material, remembering the lack of security its writers experienced.

The personal research section may help to bring the discussion down from the theoretical stratosphere!

THE BIBLE AND CONSUMERISM

Barns and butter mountains

(Have one or two people read this out.)

And Jesus said: 'There was once a rich man who had lands which produced for him fine harvests. As he considered them, he said to himself, "I have no place to keep all my crops. What should I do?"'

'He should give some of it away,' said one of the crowd. 'There's plenty would be glad of what he doesn't need.'

Jesus smiled. 'In fact the rich man did the opposite. He looked at his full barns, then called for a builder. Those great barns were pulled down to make way for even greater ones in order to store his growing wealth.'

'Greedy little devil,' muttered someone.
'He'll not enjoy all that wealth,' said another.

'Ah, you're right,' said Jesus. 'But he expected to enjoy it. He thought of all the good things he had and how he could now eat, drink and be merry . . .'

'For tomorrow we die,' chimed in a gloomy voice.

'Well,' said Jesus, 'in this story you are not so far from the truth. Except it wasn't tomorrow, it was that very night. He had time to count his wealth, he had not time to enjoy it. He was foolish enough to put his treasure where he could see it but God couldn't.'

'It's a shame the way some people hoard things for themselves,' said a middle-aged man. 'It ruins it for everyone else.'

'Of course,' said Jesus, 'the story doesn't really finish there. There were also rich countries whose lands produced fine harvests. And they met together to consider what to do.

' "We have much grain," they said. "We will store it in great silos. We have much wine, we will store it in great lakes. We will make hills of our cheese and mountains of our butter. And if we cannot get the price we want for our foods, we will destroy them." '

The crowds who listened were astonished. 'A man might be that foolish,' said one, 'but surely not many countries. Would not the poor of the world cry out? We cannot believe that such a thing has ever happened.'

'It hasn't,' said Jesus sadly, 'but it will.'

From Floods and Rainbows

Is this a fair interpretation of the parable? How have we got ourselves into this situation? What was Jesus' purpose in telling the original story? Does this updated version suggest a spiritual dimension to the problem of food mountains? How does this influence your view of the problem?

The true cost of consumerism
2 Samuel 23:13–17. David realizes that the drink cost much more than it was worth—in terms of the risk its production posed for the brave three who went for it.

He had only paid attention to the price he himself had to pay, and he had not placed any value on the price which others had to pay . . . What is at stake is the biblical rationality in calculating the cost. A product consists not only of what it costs me, but also what it costs others. According to current economic rationality, consuming can continue as long as the consumer is willing to pay this price which he or she has been charged. But that is an individualistic cost calculation . . . Biblical rationality involves the calculation of the cost before the eyes of God.

Roelf Haan in Floods and Rainbows

What does this have to say about our attitude to consumer products?

Enjoying God's blessings or relieving poverty?
The Bible seems on the one hand to encourage us to enjoy material things, but on the other to ask us to give our possessions to the poor. **2 Corinthians 8:10–15; Proverbs 30:7–9.** What is a healthy attitude towards our possessions? our income? **1 Corinthians 1:18.**

Today the language of the cross is as illogical as ever. It tells us, as it always has done, to live more simply, to share rather than accumulate, to nurture and cherish rather than to own, to live in peace and harmony even if we have to suffer for it, and at all times to acknowledge that 'All that exists comes from Him. All is by Him and for Him. To Him be the glory for ever. Amen'

Barbara Wood, Our World, God's World

Greed is a spiritual matter
Colossians 3:5–8; Exodus 16; Philippians 3:17–20; Matthew 6:31–34. Greed, overconsumption and striving for material things are seen as indications of lack of trust in God. Why is greed seen as idolatry? In what ways is a striving for material security damaging? How does the parable of the rich young man (**Matthew 19:16–26**) relate to this theme? What can we do as individuals and as a group to develop a concept of 'enough'?

Bowing before other gods
Are we to believe the prophets of ecological doom or those preaching the comforts of economic growth and prosperity? **Deuteronomy 30:15–20; Matthew 6:19–24, 7:15–20.** What are the implications of your discussion of greed and idolatry for the way we listen to the various solutions to global crisis offered by politicians and economists? How is our society influenced by false prophets and false wisdom in its pursuit of the answers to our problems? What gods do we as a society bow down to? Do you agree with Helder Camara that riches 'put scales on one's eyes'?

POPULATION EXPLOSION?

The burgeoning populations of the countries of the Third World are frequently held to blame for the energy and resources dilemmas we face. These figures for energy consumption in the USA, the UK, India and China illustrate the consumption problems we face as populations increase and the aspirations of the people of the Third World begin to be met.

Country	Population	Current energy use		Projected energy use	
		Total	Per person	Total	Per person
	(millions)	(bn m BTUs)	(m BTUs)	(bn m BTUs)	(m BTUs)
USA	232	75.1	324.0	75.1	324
UK	56	7.7	152.8	7.7	152
India	717	4.9	7.8	19.6	14
China	1008	17.9	17.8	71.6	34

The projection assumes no population growth in USA and UK, but a doubling of population and of per capita consumption in India and China. It would mean a 70 per cent increase in energy consumption in the four countries as a whole. While consumption in India and China may increase four-fold in the next thirty years, the amount they use still doesn't match that of the USA And the amount used per person is still tiny. Whose problem is energy consumption?

Which is likely to be the most effective way to reduce global warming, atmospheric pollution and the depletion of energy supplies?

◆ Controlling population increases in developing countries?

◆ Energy efficiency measures?

◆ Finding new fuel reserves?

◆ Cracking the development of the fusion reactor?

◆ Reducing consumption in the rich countries?

QUOTE VOTE

Read the following quotations and note down which you agree with, which puzzle or surprise you and which you don't go along with:

It is obvious that the world cannot afford the USA. Nor can it afford Western Europe or Japan . . . The poor don't do much damage . . . The problem passengers on Space-ship Earth are the first-class passengers and no-one else.

E.F. Schumacher

Advertising is in the business of making people helpfully dissatisfied with what they have in favour of something better. The old factors of wear and tear can no longer be depended upon to create a demand. They are too slow.

Floyd Allen, motor car executive, 1929

The earth holds enough for every man's need, not for every man's greed.

Gandhi

Greed is alright by the way. I want you to know that. You can be greedy and still feel good about yourself.

Ivan Boesky (infamous 'insider' dealer)

Again and again in the scriptures, the exploitation and suffering of the poor is directly linked to the substitution of the worship of mammon for the true worship of God.

Jim Wallis

Overconsumption is a 'cancer eating away at our spiritual vitals'. It cuts away the heart of our compassion. It distances us from the great masses of broken, bleeding humanity. It converts us into materialists. We become less able to ask moral questions.

Richard Foster

In a society like ours, the only effective way to cut down on possessions, to view what possessions we do have in a different way, to give ourselves a basic level of security while creating desirable alternatives for ourselves and our children, is to work at it within a sustaining and supporting community.

Kathleen and James McGinnis

Share your reactions as a group and, concentrating on those where your responses differ most, discuss why you responded in that way.

PERSONAL RESEARCH

One article of faith of the consumer society is that if it costs more it's worth more. This is counter to much of the teaching of Christ, but it is all around us. A few questions for personal reflection and discussion:

1 What skills do I have that I would like to share with others?

2 When was the last time I shared something I knew how to do with someone else?

3 When was the last time I learned a new skill?

4 If my children could have anything they wanted, what would they want for Christmas? Where do their desires come from?

5 How many things do I own which are worth over £200 (average annual income of the poorest third of the world's population)?

6 Outside of school, what are the three activities which involve most of my children's time? Are these activities active or passive?

7 If I were to classify my possessions into two categories—(a) those which promote self-reliance and creativity and (b) those which promote passivity and more consumption—which category would be the largest?

8 What are my 5 favourite forms of recreation? which of these costs over £1 each time I do it?

9 How much time each day do I spend watching TV? How much time each day do my children spend watching TV?

10 How many clothes do I have that I have not worn in the past year?

From Parenting for Peace and Justice

DISCUSSION

Are the best things in my life free? Do we demonstrate the truth that the abundance of life is not in the abundance of your possessions? Are people more important than things? How can we show this in our lives? Haven't we all experienced the pleasure of spending? How do we change our attitudes without seeming mean and a kill-joy?

PEOPLE OR THINGS CAN'T BUY ME LOVE

Perhaps the place where the message of Christianity contrasts most starkly with the culture of consumption is here. As a group, review the 'Action' guide and discuss what role the group/church can play in promoting the idea that what we share as a community is more important than what we own as individuals.

ACTION ON CONSUMER CULTURE

GENERAL POINTS

If our culture is too oriented towards consumption as a goal, and if we are more influenced by this than we wish to be, we can take action at various levels.

◆ Raising awareness of the ways we are influenced by the consumer society: we are largely unaware of the way our own views are manipulated by the messages we receive.

◆ Countering the negative influences on ourselves and our families: avoiding or challenging the false messages.

◆ Creating alternative influences on ourselves and society: living out better values.

ACTION IN THE HOME

The best things in life are free

The typical Western family spends more of its time with things than with people. Perhaps an unfair point, but how often do we resent guests staying on after our favourite TV programme has started? If we are to become independent of the consumer society we need to develop ways of enjoying human contact and our own creative abilities, rather than buying entertainment all the time. Having reviewed the way you use time together as a family or household, look for ways in which you can make your own entertainment. This could be:

◆ music or other artistic activity

◆ making things, such as games or decorations

◆ spending time mending or recycling broken or discarded things—perhaps for other people

◆ learning to enjoy—and care for—things that are free or held in common, such as the natural environment, libraries etc.

◆ valuing celebrations in a way that does not become a consumer orgy. *The Alternative Celebrations Catalog* is a great resource.

Making better use of the possessions we do have is part of this. Clothes and toys can be recycled through friends, plays schemes, Oxfam shops. Sharing possessions, too—a caravan, cottage or tent can be lent for holidays or escapes, perhaps for people who could not otherwise get away. A loan could be a greatly valued Christmas present! Cars and other tools represent a huge investment of resources and can be used more efficiently if shared.

Sharing your home can be a way not only of utilizing the biggest resource you have, but also of opening yourself to different world views. This can be done in a variety of ways, from short term fostering or providing 'half-way' accommodation for young people brought up in care, through to joining a network such as Servas, putting people in touch with short term accommodation in foreign countries.

Advertising

If the influence of the media on us is not all in the right direction, we can avoid contact (at least with the worst bits), but more feasibly inoculate ourselves against the undue influences. In his now classic book, *Enough is Enough*, John V. Taylor highlights the importance of this and calls for a 'joyful resistance movement' to advertising pressure in particular. He suggests that each household learns the following slogans, for chanting at the appropriate moment: 'The price tag is too high'—when we know that we don't pay the true cost of the product (cars, for example, where the enormous environmental costs are shared out); and 'Who are you kidding?' when the claims made or implied are false (can a washing powder or breakfast cereal really make us a happy family?). He also suggests that households make a pact expressly to avoid products when we are exposed to more than one advert a week for them!

Upside-down consumerism

If this is the age of consumer power, then it must be possible to turn that power around, and indeed this is what New Consumer is all about. This organization collects information about how good our big companies are as responsible citizens, and with this consumers can choose to buy from the best, and encourage companies to take other issues besides profit a bit more seriously. You can get hold of the latest information and use your resources more creatively.

Media input

One of the greatest sources of cultural values we and our children are influenced by—and the most controllable (what else has an on-off switch?)—is the television. Critically reviewing the programmes your household watches regularly could be an indispensable way of inoculating yourselves. The outline below, or the study material in the 'Resources' list, could be used by individuals or households. The basic questions to ask are, 'What views of society and relationships between people are promoted?' and, 'Why do I/we watch this programme?'

ACTION IN THE CHURCH

Within the body of the church, there is the possibility of building a 'community of resistance' to help each other (and the wider community) resist the consumer society.

Community

A commonly-held reason for our preoccupation with possessions is to make up for the lack of value we place on community; we have no other way of measuring our value. Community should also be the basis for our security. In what ways could the church develop a role in fostering community among members and more widely? Organizing days out with shared transport, a food co-op to provide good food locally at a reasonable price, a babysitting co-op with special arrangements for single parents can all help reduce reliance on consumption. Many other

ideas can come from discussion. Pools of cars, tools, books, toys, skills to be shared through the church or local community can likewise create a sense of shared community and reduce waste.

Media awareness

While it is fairly common now for people to blame at least partly pornography and violence in the media for specific anti-social behaviour, the focus tends to be on extreme behaviour of individual people. But the more subtle messages that filter through unquestioned are of greater significance. These include the sitcoms, soaps and dramas which create for us characters who define acceptable ways of doing things and an image of reality as well as the rather less subtle advertisements which tell us what we need for fulfilment.

As a group, why not spend a week monitoring TV and newspapers under one (or all) of these headings and report back your analysis?

News What sort of items take precedence? How accurate and impartial do they seem to be? Were the visual images used appropriate? What do the stories say about what is important, or what the purpose of life is?

Advertising What do adverts say about the products? What are they really selling? What images of women are portrayed? Why? Which is your favourite ad? Why? Does advertising influence you to buy something you wouldn't otherwise? What are the pros and cons of this?

Soap operas What makes them compulsive viewing? Are they offering a view of society that is accurate or desirable? How do they score on justice/morality/integrity ratings? (Philippians 4:8–9)

Children's TV List occasions when advertising aimed at children exploits links with TV series. What is the appeal of _Grange Hill_ and _Neighbours_ to children? Why is _Newsround_ popular? Could this technique be used more widely? Discuss with children what they like to see and why. How much responsibility should parents take for their children's viewing?

Monitoring your normal TV viewing Jot down all the programmes you watch for a week. Don't cheat! Note whether your viewing was planned or accidental. Categorize it by programme type. Note why you watched each. Look at the results. What is your reaction? Is your diet a balanced one in terms of spiritual growth?

Discuss: What messages do people get from the media about the society we live in, and about our goals in life? How should the church respond to this?

Why not organize some media awareness evenings along these lines?

Further action: The Mothers' Union runs a Media Awareness Project, 24 Tufton Street, London, SW1P 3RB. Christian Impact have a group Study Guide on 'Television'.

ACTION IN THE COMMUNITY

Media
While we have no call to decide for others what to watch on television or read in the papers, we do have a right and duty to express our views. Based on the results of your own survey, as well as regular reading/viewing, why not write to *Points of View, Right to Reply* or similar feedback programmes? You can also express your view to the director of the programme(s) concerned to broaden his or her views. This applies to good as well as bad programming, of course.

On broader issues of programme quality, particularly since the increasing market orientation of television has become a specific government policy, your MP is an obvious point of contact.

The Broadcasting Standards Council (5–8 The Sanctuary, London, SW1P 3JS), the Independent Broadcasting Authority (70 Brompton Road, London, SW3 1EY) are charged with maintaining standards, and should be responding to concerns outlined here, too, if only because they

represent the views of many viewers. Letters to newspapers can also be a way of encouraging reflection by other people about issues many will not have thought about before.

British Action for Children's Television, at the BFI (21 Stephen Street, London, W1P 1PL) is worth contacting for ideas on the way television can be a more positive influence on children.

While all the above might regularly receive letters about the individual moral issues, far fewer letters will focus on the concerns of this section.

Community
Some of the initiatives mentioned under 'Action in the church' are equally applicable in the wider community. Encouraging recycling and sharing is a way of reinforcing the fact that value is not all monetary, and that community life is important.

Community or publicly-owned facilities often lack people to look after them or speak up for them. The church or its members could have a role here in lobbying the council on public transport, for example, or the use to which community buildings are put. Involvement in the management of community facilities, even though this is not often seen as an avenue for church involvement, can also be a way of ensuring that community values are fostered.

ACTION IN THE WORLD

The church is worldwide, and there are many links between churches and dioceses in different countries. Such links could be a valuable way to help us become more aware of the extent to which we see Christianity through the distorting glass of our own consumerist culture. Why not discuss with your link person the possibility of inviting comment and debate on this issue from mission partners or other people based in the Third World especially?

Tourism

Tourism is a key and growing area of interaction between cultures, but rarely a helpful or creative link. Yet there is a lot that individuals can do to make the most of the opportunity to meet at a human level when on holiday in a country with a different culture from their own.

Tourism Concern is a network of people and organizations offering advice and help to people who want to concentrate on the human contact side of tourism, in the Third World especially.

The basic ideas involved in creative tourism are:

◆ finding real culture as opposed to cultural 'events' put on for tourists

◆ trying to communicate with ordinary people

◆ observing cultural norms, such as dress, so as to minimize the distance between visitor and host

◆ sensitive photography, as the camera is symbolic of the relationship in which the visitor calls the tune

◆ Buying local produce, both as an experience and to support the local community

◆ Using local transport, to meet people on common ground.

Unfortunately, most package holidays are not the ideal way to meet people, as by their nature they are all-inclusive. Escape for short periods, however, is possible and a good way to make contact.

RESOURCES

ORGANIZATIONS

New Consumer is the UK's leading public-interest organization on corporate social responsibility matters. It is a charitable foundation which derives support from individuals, educational and development charities and non-governmental groups. It monitors the social and environmental performance of Britain's major companies and undertakes major research studies. New Consumer has fostered and been engaged in the development of a wide range of social market enterprises including:

The Fairtrade Foundation - developing a guarantee mark for third world products

The Creative Consumer Co-operative - a national marketing scheme for organic produce

Shared Interest - a loan fund investing in community enterprise in the Third World

Regional environmental centres and sustainable lifestyle programmes

It offers annual membership (£15) and produces a quarterly magazine on ways consumers can support the social market and provides an advisory services to other membership organisations on responsible shopping. It has produced a series of books on these topics, all of which contain extensive practical information.

Changing Corporate Values, Kogan Page, 1991, 637pp. Rated as 'a ground breaking book in British Business Ethics,' it examines the social, environmental and ethical performance of 128 UK consumer market companies. A definitive assessment of corporate responsibility issues. Hardback £48.00 Paperback £19.95

Shopping for a Better World, Kogan Page, 1991, 288pp. A pocket guide to socially responsible shopping, rating the companies behind 2,500 popular brand names in the UK consumer market and guide to who owns what. Paperback £4.99

The Global Consumer, Victor Gollancz, 1991, 340pp. Looks at how everyday purchases can help or hinder the developing world. Paperback £7.99

The Shareholder Action Handbook, New Consumer, 1992, 160pp. A UK guide to the relationship between shareholders and directors; the range of possible constructive dialogue, pressure and direct action, and legal background, information sources and resources available. Paperback £5.95

Britain's Best Employers?, Kogan Page, 1993, 340pp. This is the first book published in the UK to provide job hunters with impartial advice and information across the entire range of business, social and ethical activities of the country's major graduate employers, in both the public and private sectors. It includes, but moves beyond, the concerns of pay and conditions in rating employers. Paperback £10.95

Good Business, SAUS Publications, 1993, 142pp. Eleven case detailed case studies in business corporate responsibility with supporting comment on management theory. Paperback £13.50

All these books are available in good bookshops or post free directly from: New Consumer, 52 Elswick Road, Newcastle upon Tyne, NE4 6JH. Tel. 091 272 1148.

The Lifestyle Movement provides a Christian perspective on living simply that others may simply live. 1, Manor Farm, Little Gidding, Cambs. PE17 5RJ.

New Economics Foundation explores issues of contemporary economics and social living from the perspective of the need to prevent environmental degradation and global inequities. A quarterly magazine and numerous study papers are available to members (£15 per annum). NEF, 88/94 Wentworth Street, London, E1 7SA.

ACTION/DISCUSSION MATERIAL

Debt Trap Action Bible study on attitudes to debt and wealth. From Jubilee Centre, 3 Hooper Street, Cambridge CB1 2NZ.

Credit and debt—sorting it out Information, advice and case studies on getting back to financial control after debt. £2.99. From Jubilee Centre.

Freedom of Simplicity Richard Foster. An expansion of this theme from his spiritual classic *Celebration of Discipline.* Triangle/SPCK.

Floods and Rainbows A study guide from the Methodist Church, mainly about the environment, but has relevant material. Methodist Publishing House, 20 Ivatt Way, Westwood, Peterborough PE3 7PG.

Our World, God's World Barbara Wood. With its main focus on the environment, this book is full of relevant reflections and readings. Bible Reading Fellowship.

Christian Impact Study Series: *TV* looks at one of the most potent cultural influences and how it is controlled. From Christian Impact Publications, 79 Maid Marian Way, Nottingham NG1 6AE.

Parenting for Peace and Justice Kathleen and James McGinnis. Referred to in several places in this book, it is a practical guide to encouraging positive values through family life. Orbis Publishing.

Alternative Celebrations Catalog A wonderful collection of ways to celebrate anything witout consuming the earth. An American publication, but you might find a copy in 'alternative' bookshops or libraries.

Born to Shop Mike Starkey, Monarch Publications. A readable—and in parts lighthearted—review of consumer culture, the media and Christian values.

OTHER TRAINING BOOKS FROM LYNX COMMUNICATIONS

The World Christian
Robin Thompson

This workbook is intended for anyone wanting to learn how to be a real modern missionary: one who crosses from culture to culture with sensitivity and awareness, understanding the gospel well enough to interpret it for people of quite different worldviews. The course was developed by St John's Extension Studies, Nottingham.

ISBN 0 7459 2540 5

£10.50

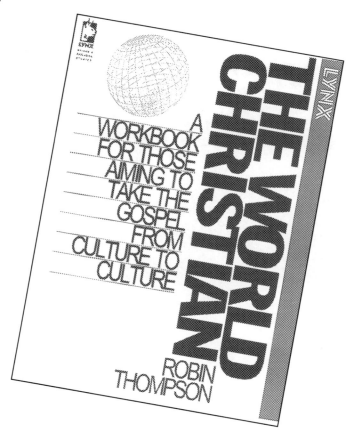

An Introduction to Church Communication
Richard Thomas

This second title in the Lynx training format is written by the Communications Officer of the Oxford Diocese, and founder of the Churches Media Trust. He has provided just the training book needed by ministers and publicity officers of churches who want to project a good image to their local communities.

ISBN 0 7459 2886 2
£10.00
Publishing April 1994

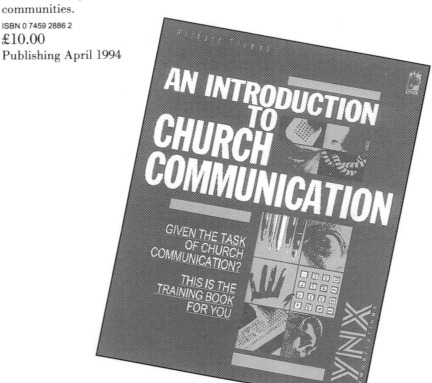

Available from your bookshop, or direct from:

Lynx Communications,
Peter's Way,
Sandy Lane West,
Oxford,
OX4 5HG,
England.

or fax with your credit card number:

UK: (0865) 747568
International: +44 865 747568

Add for postage & packing:

£3 (UK)
£5 (Europe)
£7 (Rest of World)